Fun & Fabulous Curtains to Sew

15 Easy Designs for the Complete Beginner

Fun & Fabulous

Curtains to Sew

15 Easy Designs for the Complete Beginner

Valerie Van Arsdale Shrader

LARK BOOKS
A Division of Sterling Publishing Co., Inc.
New York

ART DIRECTOR:
Stacey Budge
COVER DESIGNER:
Barbara Zaretsky
ASSOCIATE EDITOR:
Nathalie Mornu
ASSOCIATE ART DIRECTOR:
Shannon Yokeley
ART PRODUCTION ASSISTANT:
Jeff Hamilton
EDITORIAL ASSISTANCE:
Delores Gosnell
ILLUSTRATOR:
Bernadette Wolf
PHOTOGRAPHER:
Stewart O'Shields

Library of Congress Cataloging-in-Publication Data

Shrader, Valerie Van Arsdale, 1956-
Fun & fabulous curtains to sew : 15 easy designs for the complete beginner / Valerie Van Arsdale Shrader. -- 1st ed.
p. cm.
Includes index.
ISBN 1-57990-794-6 (hardcover)
1. Draperies. 2. Sewing. I. Title. II. Title: Fun and fabulous curtains to sew.
TT390.S45 2006
646.2'1--dc22
2006020097

10 9 8 7 6 5 4 3 2 1

First Edition

Published by Lark Books, A Division of
Sterling Publishing Co., Inc.
387 Park Avenue South, New York, N.Y. 10016

Distributed in Canada by Sterling Publishing,
c/o Canadian Manda Group, 165 Dufferin Street
Toronto, Ontario, Canada M6K 3H6

Distributed in the United Kingdom by GMC Distribution Services,
Castle Place, 166 High Street, Lewes, East Sussex, England BN7 1XU

Distributed in Australia by Capricorn Link (Australia) Pty Ltd.,
P.O. Box 704, Windsor, NSW 2756 Australia

If you have questions or comments about this book, please contact:
Lark Books
67 Broadway
Asheville, NC 28801
(828) 253-0467

Manufactured in China

ISBN 13: 978-1-57990-794-5
ISBN 10: 1-57990-794-6

For information about custom editions, special sales, premium and corporate purchases, please contact Sterling Special Sales Department at 800-805-5489 or specialsales@sterlingpub.com.

Contents

Make a Curtain!

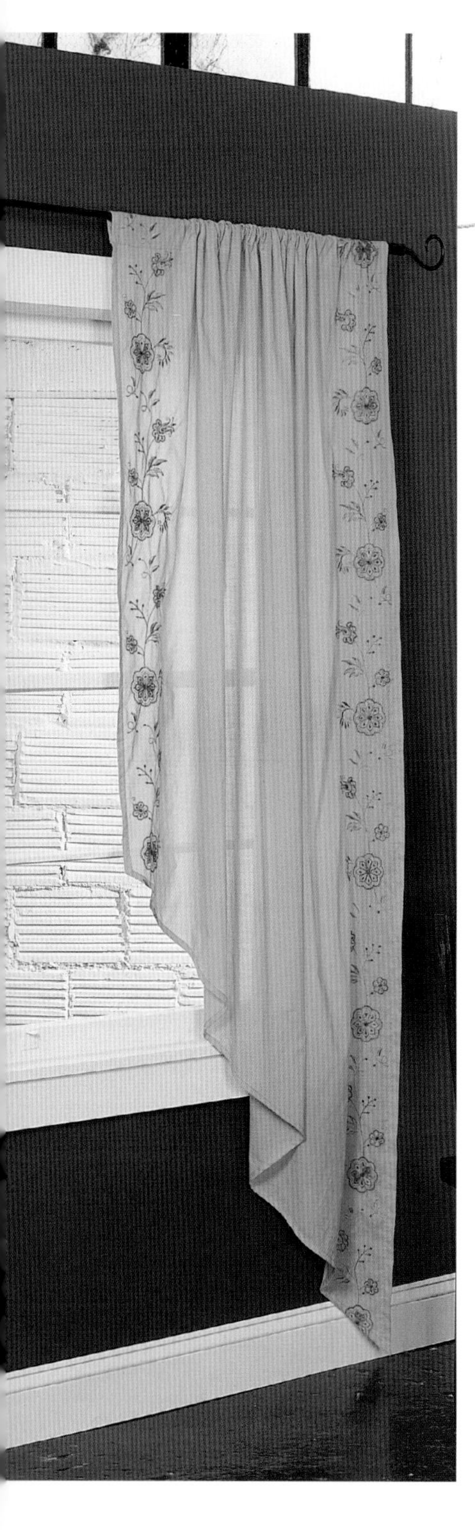

Introduction

You know what a curtain call is, of course. It's that triumphant time at the end of a production when the cast comes out to receive their just rewards, a hearty round of applause for a job well done. Well, look around the room—if your curtains came out for a hand, would they get it?

Hmmm. Let's study your house. You bought the curtains in the living room because the color was good, but the length is a little off. No applause for them. In the bedroom, the dark curtains provide a lot of privacy, but they don't let in *any* light. And the bathroom? Well, a plain ol' shade from the home improvement center does the job, but it's certainly not exciting. No bravos for these rooms, either.

Suppose you wanted your window treatments to inspire a standing ovation. You could hire a designer to dress your windows perfectly, if money were no object. But let's get real: since money *is* a consideration, how about buying some ready-made curtains instead? Chances are you'll still end up paying beaucoup bucks for curtains that are *almost* the right color and *almost* the right length. Here's an idea—why not become a decorator and make your own window treatments? Then you'll always have the perfect curtains for your rooms, and you'll always stay within your budget (which means money left over for the truly important things in life, like shoes).

Seriously now, if you've been leery of sewing before, this is the perfect opportunity to learn. Curtains are just about the simplest thing you could ever make, and they're also easy to embellish and personalize. And when I'm talking window treatments, I'm not talking fancy draperies with lining and weights and pinch pleats and...ugh. I'm talking about hip curtains, easy to make and easy to love, with contemporary deconstructed details like raw edges. Most of our projects are simple and unlined, and all were designed to be within the reach of the beginner sewer.

Speaking of sewing, we'll take you through the entire process, starting with all the basic techniques. Our illustrated projects let you see how easy it is to make the curtains in this book. And what's more, we won't clutter up your mind with information that you don't need, because we're going to focus strictly on the techniques you need to make beautiful window treatments. Of course, all of these techniques can be used in other types of sewing, too, just in case you get inspired to make a pillow or maybe a skirt (and we're sure you will).

In *Fun & Fabulous Curtains to Sew,* we've included 15 projects to dress your windows, including curtains, simple drapes, café curtains, shades, and more. These treatments will create atmosphere in your room, and they're decorative and functional, as they provide privacy, filter sunlight, and accent your furnishings. You'll learn how to adorn your windows with style and add unique touches to your living space. And don't forget that you'll learn a valuable new skill to add to your DIY repertoire.

Well, what are you waiting for? When you've finished making your own fabulous curtains, there will be plenty of applause, I'm sure. Let's begin, shall we?

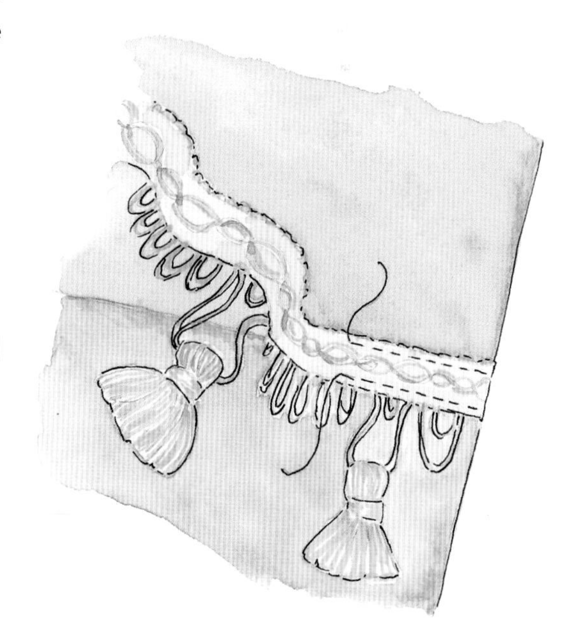

Guide to Making Fabulous Curtains

There's a curtain to fit every window, of course, whether you've got modern sliding windows or funky sash windows. Your first decision will be the kind of window treatment you want, so let's consider the variables: Do you want to provide privacy? Allow some light filtration, but screen out a boring view? Provide some spark in a drab room? Supply additional insulation? Keep in mind that your window treatments should match the character of your room, yet provide an opportunity to express your personal style. While you're thinking about those questions, here's some information about window treatments.

Pick a type

At its most basic, a curtain is a piece of fabric that's hemmed on all four sides and hung with clips. There's a difference between *curtains* and *draperies;* while curtains are generally unlined, draperies are lined with an additional layer of fabric, and sometimes have a third layer of interlining fabric. Most of the projects in this book, you'll be delighted to hear, can be defined as curtains. This simple shape can be transformed by way of adding headers, tabs, ties, embellishments—once you understand the basics, you can apply your creativity to the form. Let's look at some common types.

ROD POCKET. This basic curtain hangs from the rod by way of a casing, also called a rod pocket. Using a perky fabric for this simple curtain can add a spark to the room, and no one will have to know how easy it is to make. (We certainly won't tell!) Coupled with a distinctive curtain rod, this window treatment is a good choice for a quick room makeover.

Rod pocket

How do I make thee? Let me count the ways.

ROD POCKET WITH HEADER. To take the basic curtain one step further, add one more line of stitching to create a decorative header above the rod. A header will add another few inches of curtain to your room, offering you the opportunity to enjoy your fabric a bit more.

VALANCE. The valance is a short little curtain that hangs at the top of a window. It can soften the bare window frame, while not screening out light or a fabulous view.

CAFÉ. The opposite of the valance, this is a short little curtain that covers only the bottom half of the window. It allows light in, but also provides some privacy. This curtain is easily hung with a tension rod, which makes installation a breeze.

TAB TOP. As an alternative to a casing, you can add tabs at the top of your curtain. And a variation on this style would be to use ties, rather than tabs. Either of these methods can be used if you want a more casual look.

Rod pocket with header

Valance

Café

Tab top & tie top

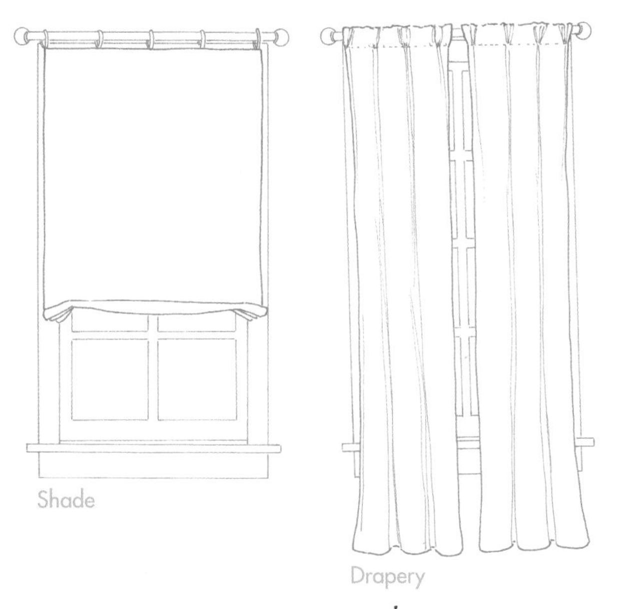

SHADE. A shade can cover all or part of a window, depending on your needs, and takes relatively little fabric to make. Although technically not a curtain, we think any book on window treatments ought to have one or two super-easy shades—don't you?

DRAPERY. In this book, we have a set of draperies that are lined and involve some more sophisticated construction than our curtains. But fear not—we'll teach you all the skills you need to make these stylish window treatments. When you're looking for an uptown look, consider making some draperies.

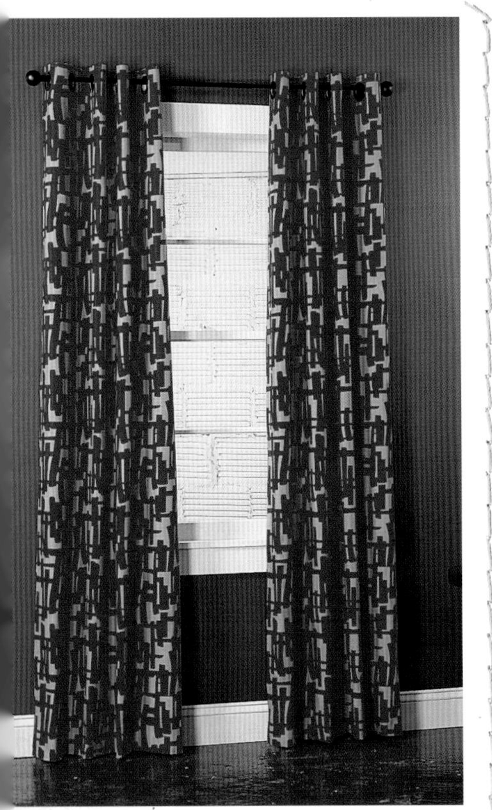

Floor-length curtains like this should skim just above the floor.

Choose a length

Just as there are different categories of window treatments, there are also reasons to make your curtains different lengths, the most important of which is your own aesthetic. Some other reasons are practical—if you've got a radiator underneath your window, you probably don't want your curtains so long they cover up your heat source *or* become a fire hazard. Generally, you'll find that more formal window treatments are often floor-length, while more casual styles are usually shorter.

There are some general guidelines for curtain lengths. We just discussed valances (on the upper part of the window) and café curtains (on the lower part of the window), but note there are three other lengths. Sill length can range from about ½ inch above the sill to the bottom of the framework; apron length can fall from the bottom of the framework to 6 inches below the framework; and full-length curtains should drape to roughly ½ inch above the floor. If you want your window treatments to puddle on the floor, make them longer than floor length, up to a foot longer if you'd like. (Pet lovers, beware: your furry friends may enjoy playing with your ultra-long curtains.)

Choose a width

Just as there are general notions for the length of a curtain, there are similar ideas about curtain width. This refers to how full the curtain will be. Recommendations vary slightly, so we'll offer you a range of options.

Tailored curtains are the same width as the window; standard curtains are from one and one-half to two times the width of the window; and full curtains are two to three times the width of the window. The figures are also somewhat dependent on the fabric you choose; a sheer fabric can be gathered to a greater degree than heavy linen can, for example. To simplify matters (which is what we're all about, remember), we used the formulas you see in the box when we made our projects. You'll see the fullness icons that refer to these formulas (1X, 1.5X, 2X) again in the instructions that accompany our lovely curtains.

When we discuss measuring on page 17, you'll also see a helpful illustration about length and width.

Tailored	1X	same width as the window
Standard	1.5X	one and one-half times the width of the window
Full	2X	two times the width of the window

Choose a heading

After you've got a basic idea about the style of your curtain, you should decide what kind of heading you want. The terms *header* or *heading* refer to the top of the curtain, the area of the curtain that will be attached to the curtain rod or pole. These terms can also refer specifically to the decorative fabric that extends above the casing (figure 1), and you'll probably find the terms used interchangeably. (In other words, the curtain experts disagree on the definitions.)

For our purposes, tabs, ties, pleats, casings, etc., will all be considered types of headings. A heading can be as plain as a simple rod pocket casing, or as elaborate as a series of triple pleats. The latter are created rather simply by using special tapes that create all sorts of lovely effects, as you'll see below. If your taste tends to the classic or formal, you may want to investigate these products. But if your taste tends to the funky, headings can also be embellished with ribbon or fringe, because the header is the perfect canvas on which to play. We'll learn to make the basic types of headings when we Learn to Sew! on page 27. (I can't wait!)

FIGURE 1. A decorative header

For an elegant look, use silk fabric and pleating tape to create this formal heading.

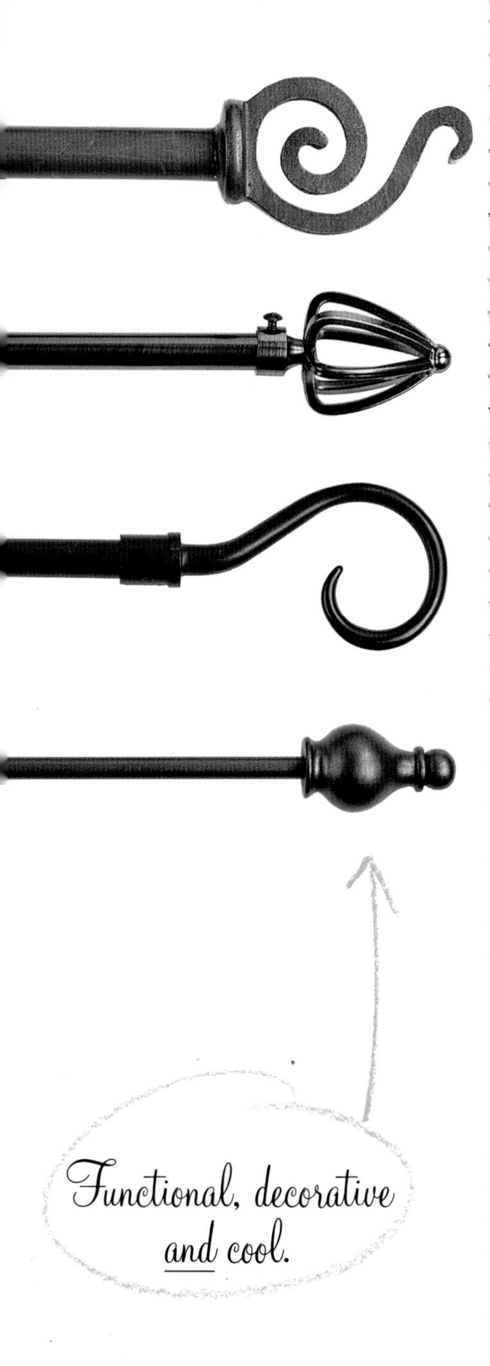

Buy your hardware

For the greatest accuracy, it helps to have the hardware in place when you measure for your window treatment project. (We'll learn how to measure on page 17.) We've used fairly straightforward rods for most of our projects, again with simplicity and ease in mind. It makes sense to have the hardware before you begin to make your curtains for several other reasons, too. The diameter of the rod itself is important if you're making curtains with a rod pocket and/or header, because that will affect the length of your curtains—as well as how they fit the rod. We'll talk about this some more on page 18.

There are decorative considerations as well. Even though the selection of hardware is huge, maybe it's not as huge as you thought. What I'm trying to say is this: Don't assume the perfect hardware will be there *after* you've already invested time and money in your window treatments. If the color and style of the hardware is vitally important to your overall vision, buy it first so it becomes part of the planning process for your curtain projects. While you can extrapolate and say, "Well, I know I'll put the rod 2 inches above the window," it's really best to mount it first.

We're not interior designers around here, but here's an interesting idea about the placement of your window treatments. A well-conceived placement can affect the proportions of a room. For example, if your room is small or the ceiling is low, hang floor-length curtains high above the window, because it will make the room seem bigger. So, give some thought to the optimum placement of your window treatments before you make the first stitch.

Choose your fabric

Now, let's turn our attention to the important subject of the fabric. I promise not to bore you to death with lots of information, but as a responsible author (and fabric junkie), I feel obligated to share some knowledge. And you know what? Even the most outrageously easy-to-make curtain can look extraordinary when you choose the right fabric.

A little general background first. Fabrics can be woven or knit, and are made of fibers of various origins. Since you're interested in sewing, you probably already have a basic knowledge of the different types of fabric and what they're made from: the natural fibers, such as cotton, linen, wool, and silk; and the synthetic fibers, like polyester, acrylic, and nylon. (Isn't chemistry wonderful?) Rayon straddles these two categories, as it's synthesized from wood pulp; it's manmade, yet from a natural source. Other synthetic fabrics are made from sources such as petroleum products, and many fabrics are blends of natural and synthetic fibers.

Each bolt of fabric in the store will be labeled with its fiber content, its width, its price, and occasionally its laundering requirements. Now, the mention of the word "launder" brings up another important question about your curtains—every now and then, they're going to need to be cleaned. This factor directly relates to the kind of fabric that would be most appropriate for your window treatments, and it also relates to the all-important pocketbook. Most silks, as you probably know, need to be professionally cleaned. So, do you want to be able to wash the curtains yourself, or are you willing to pay to have them dry-cleaned? Be sure to ask about laundering the fabric before you buy it, so you understand how you must care for your curtains after you've made them. Washable fabrics need to be preshrunk before being sewn, which simply means laundering

them according to the manufacturer's recommendations before you start to sew. (Don't worry; we're going to go through the whole process step-by-step in just a few pages.)

If a fabric is woven, its weave gives it specific characteristics. Satin, velvet, twill, and so on describe the structure of the fabric and not its fiber content. Velvet can be made from silk, cotton, or polyester, for example. The only types of fabric that should be avoided in making curtains are those that are very stiff, because they won't drape well. For a happy sewing experience, consider using cotton fabric for your first project because it handles and washes well, it's durable, and it's easy to sew. Cotton is also relatively inexpensive, and this is not an unimportant consideration: depending on the style of window treatment you choose, you could need many (perhaps *many*) yards of fabric.

FIGURE 2. In most cases, the length of the fabric will flow down the window in one continuous piece. You may occasionally add additional width (indicated by the dashed line) for a wide window treatment.

When you're shopping, you've got two choices. You can look in a shop that specializes in dressmaking goods, or you can visit a store that offers decorator fabrics for home décor applications. There are wonderful fabrics to be had at each type of shop. Dressmaking fabrics (also called fashion fabrics) are usually folded lengthwise and wrapped around a cardboard bolt. Decorator fabrics are usually left unfolded—so the entire width is on display—and rolled in all their glory onto a tube.

A major difference between the two types of fabric is the width; most dressmaking fabrics are 44 or 45 inches wide, while decorator fabrics are 54 or even 60 inches wide. This extra width could be significant, as a few more inches of width could prevent you from having to buy lots of additional fabric. For example, if you're dressing a very wide window, and you want a full curtain, dressmaking fabric may not be wide enough to span the width, so you would have to stitch two widths of fabric together. Since fabric is sold by the length, not the width, you still have to buy enough additional yardage for the entire length, even if you only need a few extra inches of width (figure 2). And, decorator fabrics are also designed for use in the home, so they can be very durable.

Consider the fabric's weight when you're shopping. A lightweight, sheer fabric will allow some natural light while camouflaging a less-than-perfect view, while a heavyweight fabric will help insulate and block out light, providing more privacy, if that's what you're after. (And let's face it, some of us do want more privacy.) It's a good idea to get swatches of the fabrics that interest you and take them home so you can hold them up to the window you're going to decorate. This is helpful for a couple of reasons: the sunlight may have an effect on the fabric, perhaps making it appear more sheer, and the light will probably affect the density of the color, too. You may consider buying just enough fabric (a 1/4 yard) to practice sewing with it, too, to be sure you and the fabric are compatible.

Design your window treatment

Now that we've talked about form and function, let's get down to the nitty-gritty and plan your window treatment. Then, we'll figure out your yardage requirements so you can buy fabric, and then we start sewing! The fun will soon begin. Here's a little list of things to think about.

Style

Length

Fullness

Heading

Fabric

Okay. You've got a couple of windows that desperately need some excitement. Your style is casual, with some bohemian elements tossed in for drama. You're a beginning sewer, so how about a simple pair of rod-pocket curtains? This decision covers both the style and the heading, too. A cool fabric, maybe an interesting print, will add just the touch your room needs.

So, how about the length? Floor-length curtains are probably a bit formal for you. And sill length will leave some of the window framework exposed, and it's not what you might call beautiful. Let's consider apron length, which will cover the window frame. Perfect.

Next, we'll consider the fullness. You probably want a little romance, so your lovely fabric can billow about with the spring breeze. Let's decide on a standard width, which is one and one-half times the width of the window. The fabric will cover your window with some extra fullness to spare.

As to the heading, we're going to keep it simple for this first project, so we already picked a simple rod pocket, or casing, for the header. So our final decision becomes the fabric. After a delightful afternoon of browsing fabric stores, we decided on a lovely cotton print, with paisley and flower motifs. Our swatch looked fabulous when we displayed in on our window, with the light illuminating the print. We loved it! So now we figure out how much fabric to buy. Please put your thinking caps on for a few minutes while we talk yardage.

Calculating yardage requirements

Now that you've decided what kind of window treatment you want, it's time to buy your fabric. To purchase the proper amount of fabric for your windows, you have to do some measuring and some figuring. (Yes, this means a little math. But it's not hard. Trust me.) The yardage you'll need will depend upon several factors, including the finished length of the curtain, the fullness of your curtain, and the width of the curtain rod.

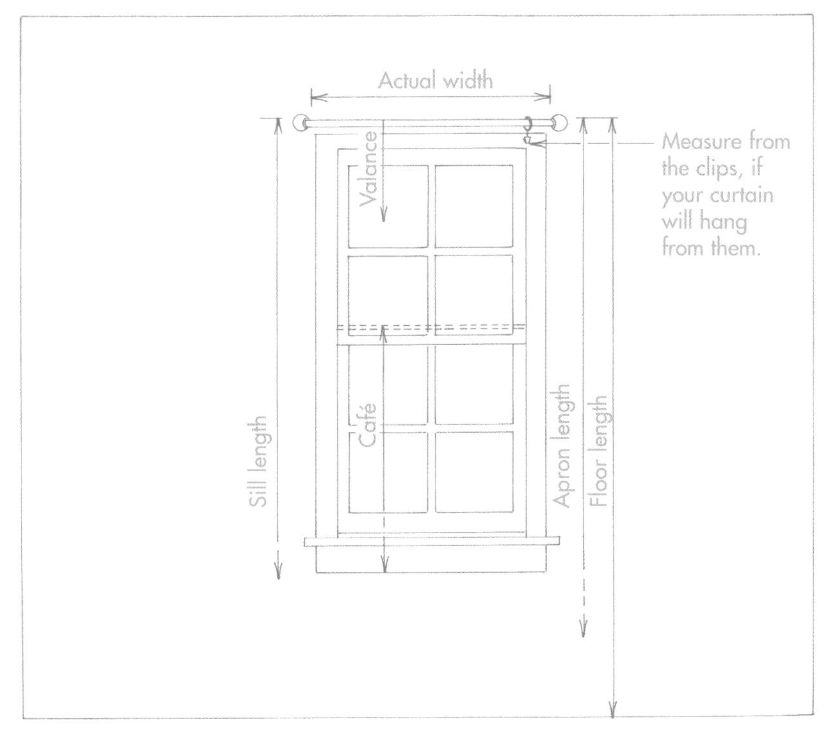

FIGURE 3. Here are the areas to measure, including some common curtain lengths. You should measure for the length from the top of the rod (unless your curtain will hang from drapery clips), and measure the width between the finials, from bracket to bracket. Variations in length are indicated by dashes at the ends of the lines.

Measuring

As we mentioned earlier, it's best to have the rod in place before you measure, because you've got to factor in its placement when you plan your curtains. There are no real rules for placing the rods (and if there were, we wouldn't care, would we?). Current wisdom suggests that the brackets should be mounted about 2 to 4 inches above the window frame and from 2 to 4 inches on either side. Feel free to use your best judgment, however, and install the rods where you think they'll look best.

If possible, use a locking metal tape measure for the greatest accuracy. Measure from the rod to the desired length, or drop, of your curtain; if you're planning to attach your curtains with clips, hang a clip onto the rod and measure from the bottom of the clip, not the rod. If you're making floor-length curtains, you may want to measure at several spots along the width of the window, as the window may not be completely plumb, or your floor may not be exactly level. For the width, measure the rod from bracket to bracket, not the window, unless you plan to mount your curtains inside the window frame. And if you're dressing more than one window in a room, measure each window, even if you think they're all the same size.

Figure 3 details the areas to measure. Next, we'll figure out some yardage so you can see how it's done.

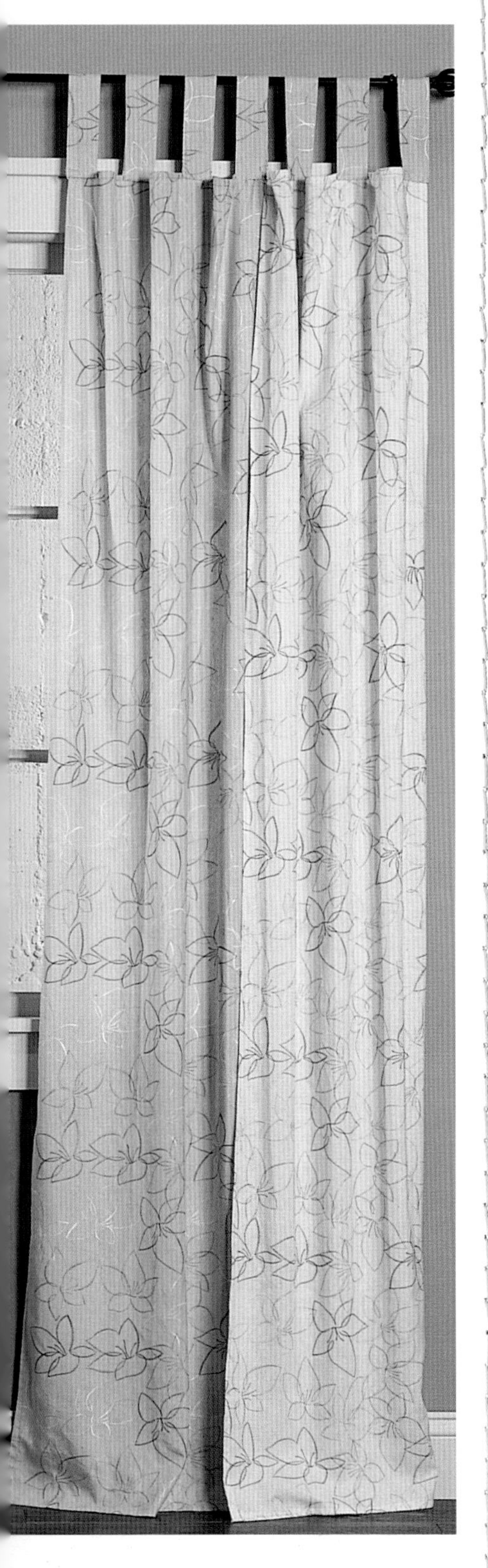

Calculating

We're going to use the same rod-pocket curtain we planned on page 16 as an example in this little exercise. Let's figure the length first, as it's quite straightforward.

1 We measured from the top of the rod to our desired finished length, which is the bottom of the sill (55 inches).

2 Now, to the finished length, we added an allowance for the rod pocket (3 inches).

3 Next, we added an allowance for the hem (6 inches).

4 We totaled these figures for our cut length (64 inches).

5 Because we plan to have a rod pocket header, we need to allow for the diameter of the rod, which will cause our curtain to be a little shorter. This is called the *take-up allowance*. If your hem length is critical (for instance, if you want to have your curtains hit just at the edge of the sill, as we did), you'll need to factor in the take-up distance. Add the diameter of the rod (5/8 inches, in our case) to your length (so our total is 64 5/8 inches). If your hem length can vary a little, you don't have to worry about the take-up distance.

*Now, to the width,
which involves a little more figuring.*

6 Next, we measured the width from bracket to bracket (53 inches).

7 We divided this figure by the number of panels we want, which is two (53÷2 = 26 1/2 inches).

8 We decided to use the standard fullness (1.5X) for this project, so we multiplied the standard fullness by the actual width of

each panel ($1\frac{1}{2} \times 26\frac{1}{2}$ inches = $39\frac{3}{4}$ inches), and rounded up to the next whole number (40 inches).

9 We then added on the additional allowances for the side hems, 4 inches on each side of each panel. So we added 8 inches to the width of each panel to reach our cut width for each panel (40 + 8 = 48 inches).

10 To calculate our yardage, we need the total width for our curtain, so we'll multiply by 2, since we have two panels (48 x 2 = 96 inches).

Okay—just about done!

11 We divided our total cut width (96 inches) by the width of our fabric ($96 \div 54 = 1\frac{4}{5}$ widths).

12 We rounded up the figure from step 11 to 2 widths. (Always round up, people, because you can't buy less than a full width of fabric.)

13 Finally, we multiplied the number of widths we needed (2) by the length we needed ($64\frac{5}{8}$ inches) to figure our total fabric requirement ($2 \times 64\frac{5}{8} = 129\frac{1}{4}$ inches).

14 To figure yardage, we divided $129\frac{1}{4}$ inches by 36 (a bit over $3\frac{1}{2}$ yards). To be on the safe side, we rounded up to have a little extra fabric, so we purchased 4 yards of cotton.

15 From our 4 yards, we'll cut two panels that are each 48 inches wide (from step 9) x $64\frac{5}{8}$ inches long (from step 5).

Use the chart at the right to calculate your fabric needs. If you're putting a very full curtain on a super-wide window, you'll need to stitch widths of fabric together. If so, add an extra inch of fabric in step 9 for each seam you need.

Now, on to the sewing machine!

Fabric Calculator

	______	**1.** FINISHED LENGTH
+	______	**2.** HEADER
+	______	**3.** LOWER HEM
	______	**4.** CUT LENGTH PER PANEL
+	______	**5.** TAKE-UP ALLOWANCE *(if applicable)*
	______	TOTAL CUT LENGTH
	______	**6.** WIDTH OF CURTAIN *(bracket to bracket)*
÷	______	**7.** NUMBER OF PANELS
	______	WIDTH PER PANEL
X	______	**8.** DESIRED FULLNESS
	______	TOTAL FULLNESS PER PANEL
+	______	**9.** SIDE HEMS
	______	CUT WIDTH PER PANEL
X	______	**10.** NUMBER OF PANELS
	______	TOTAL CUT WIDTH
÷	______	**11.** FABRIC WIDTH
	______	**12.** TOTAL WIDTHS NEEDED *(round up)*
X	______	**13.** TOTAL CUT LENGTH
	______	TOTAL FABRIC NEEDED
÷	36	**14.** INCHES PER YARD
	______	TOTAL YARDAGE NEEDED

15. DIMENSION OF EACH CUT PANEL

Meet the Sewing Machine

The next step is to develop a meaningful relationship with your sewing machine, since it's the tool that allows you to make fabulous curtains. Give it a friendly little pat and let's get to know it better. Later, when we Learn to Sew! on page 27, we'll discuss some of its functions in greater detail. I love my sewing machine! I really do.

How it works

This fantastic invention creates a lockstitch when the thread from the needle (on top of the machine) and the thread from the bobbin (inside the machine) loop together in the fabric. This happens a gazillion times per minute when you sew. (Aren't you glad you don't have to do it by hand? I sure am.) That's the long, the short, and the zigzag of it.

Although machines share common characteristics, they vary by manufacturer. When I keep referring you to your own machine's manual, I'm not trying to ignore your needs; it's because there are some subtle yet important differences between machines that might confuse you. For instance, the thread on my machine disappears inside for part of its journey—yours might not. My bobbin winds on the front of the machine—yours might be on top. I have a pressure foot dial, but you might have a lever. Despite that rambling disclaimer, I'm going to give you some general information about sewing machines. Let's give it a whirl.

See the illustration on the opposite page: a typical machine has a spool (or spools) for the thread; controls for stitch width, stitch length, thread tension, and presser foot pressure (say that three times fast); a handwheel; a take-up lever; tension disks; a presser foot lever; thread guides; a bobbin winder; a needle; a presser foot; feed dogs; a needle plate; and a bobbin. All of these things furiously work together to create the little lockstitch that makes your curtain. Most modern machines have a detachable accessory tray that's part of the sewing surface;

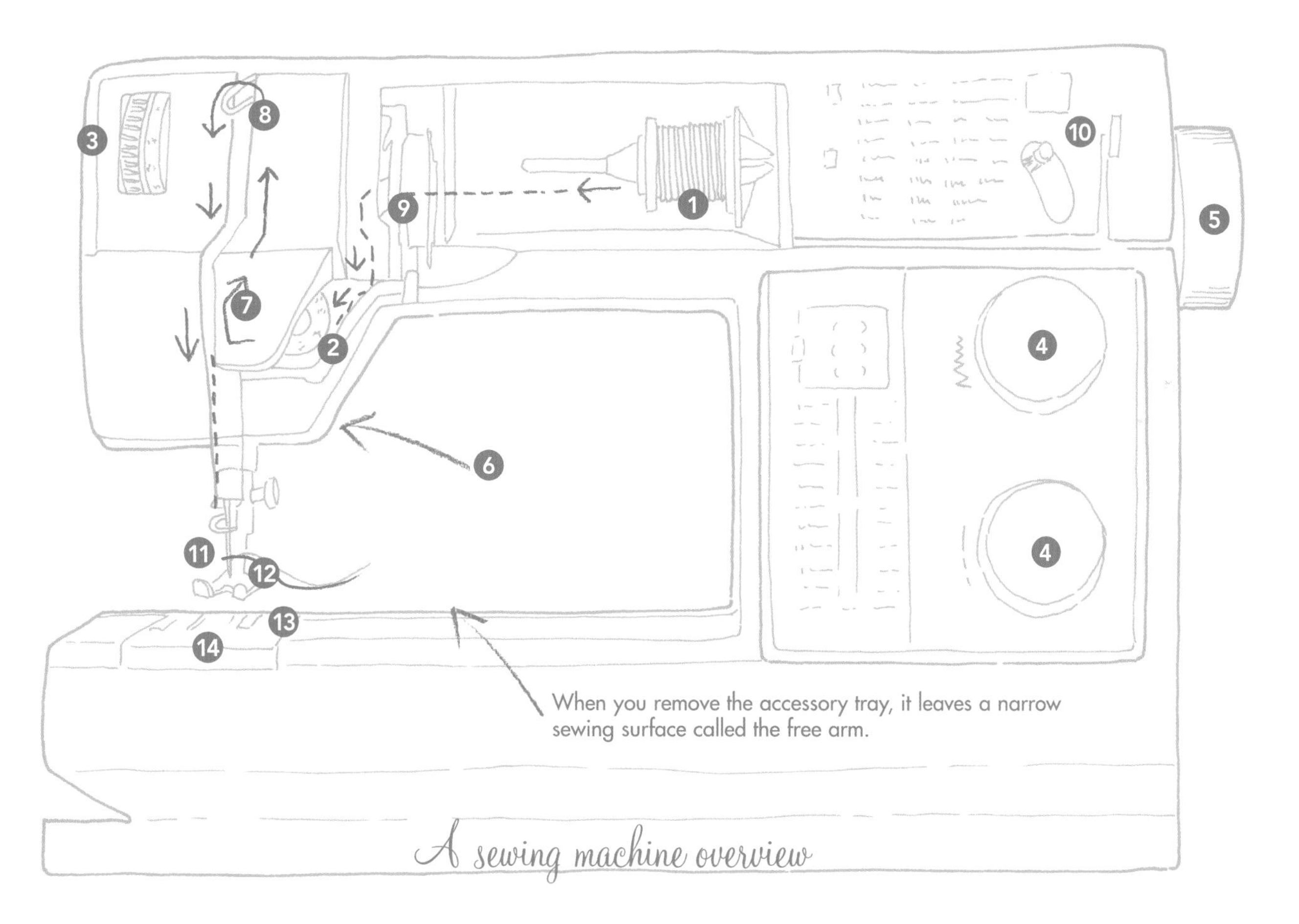

1. The spool holds the hread.

2. This dial adjusts the hread tension; turn it in tiny ncrements.

3. Adjust the pressure of he presser foot with this dial.

4. These dials adjust stitch selection, including width and length.

5. The handwheel revolves when you sew, and you can urn it by hand for precision work.

6. The presser foot lever (hiding in the back) lifts the presser foot and engages the tension disks. Remember to put it in the down position when you sew! But *lift* the presser foot when you thread your machine.

7. The tension disks, tucked inside the machine, regulate the movement of the thread.

8. The take-up lever carries the thread while the machine is sewing, pulling the exact amount it needs for each stitch. If this lever isn't threaded properly, an unsightly gob of thread will appear on your fabric.

9. The thread guides move the thread through the machine in an orderly fashion.

10. The bobbin winder winds the thread on the bobbin, of course.

11. The needle pierces the fabric and creates a stitch when it's looped together with the thread from the bobbin. Use the right size needle for your fabric, and use a new needle for each project.

12. The presser foot keeps the fabric snug against the feed dogs, the little serrated thingies that move the fabric as you sew.

13. The needle plate is the metal surface through which the needle grabs the bobbin thread. It has handy guidelines for seam allowances.

14. The bobbin is wound with thread and lives inside the machine. The looping of the thread from the spool with the thread from the bobbin forms the basic lockstitch.

when it's removed, a narrow sewing surface called a *free arm* remains. The free arm lets you stitch inside pieces that are narrow, should you ever need to do so.

In case you could have possibly forgotten (!), your sewing machine manual is the best source of information for your particular model. It will have detailed information about threading the machine; winding the bobbin; adjusting stitch width and length; and selecting any specialty stitches. Read through the manual thoroughly before you begin to make your curtain and practice stitching to familiarize yourself with the operation of your machine. It will be fun!

Use the right needle

There's no great mystery to choosing the proper needle for your curtain. The three major types are sharps, for use on finely woven fabrics; ballpoints, for knits; and universal points, for all-purpose sewing on both knits and woven fabrics. Needles come in different sizes, with the smaller numbers for use on lightweight fabrics and the larger numbers for heavyweight material. They are marked in both European (60, 70, etc.) and American (10, 12, and so on) sizes; which number comes first depends on the manufacturer. A universal point in the medium range (80/12, for instance) will suit most of the fabric used in this book.

Use the right presser foot

The presser foot is the gizmo that keeps the fabric secure against the feed dogs; the feed dogs are the gizmos that move the fabric along as you sew. There are lots of specialized presser feet designed to perform specific tasks, but we keep it simple in this book by primarily using only the general presser foot, which allows both straight and zigzag stitching. When you start making garments (No, I don't have any ulterior motives!), you'll also use the zipper foot, which lets you stitch close to the zipper when you're installing it. There are also specialized zipper feet for putting in an invisible zipper, adding piping, etc. That handy manual of yours will instruct you on changing the presser feet.

Got Sewing Machine?

If you already have a sewing machine, you're ready to make a curtain. But, please hear this: The machine is really, really important, because if it doesn't operate properly, you won't be able to sew successfully. And you won't make any fabulous curtains.

1 You don't have to spend a ton of money to get a per-ectly good entry-level sewing nachine. But you really should jo to a dealer and test-drive pefore you buy. Sew over dif-erent thicknesses of fabric, hread it yourself, wind the pobbin, check out the stitch election, make a button-ole—dealers expect and wel-come this level of scrutiny rom their customers. Many dealers offer an introductory class after you've purchased a nachine.

2 If you buy a used machine, insist on that test-drive, too. Stitching can look dread-fully wonky when there's actual-ly not much wrong (maybe just a tension adjustment on the bobbin), but then again, maybe that poor machine has been abused. Have a rep-utable dealer inspect it before you plunk down your hard-earned cash. Make sure that you have a complete operating manual, too.

3 If you borrow a machine, please don't make the mistake of hauling a dusty machine out of someone's attic and thinking it will sew beautifully. Maybe it will, but probably it won't; sewing machines need to be tuned up regularly, just like cars. They work awfully hard, and they accumulate lots of dust from fabric and thread. (This dust migrates into the screwiest places, too.) Get a proper introduction from the machine's owner (do a lot of the same things I suggest when you're shopping for a machine) and have the owner point out its important fea-tures. Don't forget to borrow that manual, also. (As if!)

Gather the Tools and Supplies

In addition to the sewing machine, you'll need to get a few other tools and materials before you begin your first curtain. All of these items are readily available at any fabric shop.

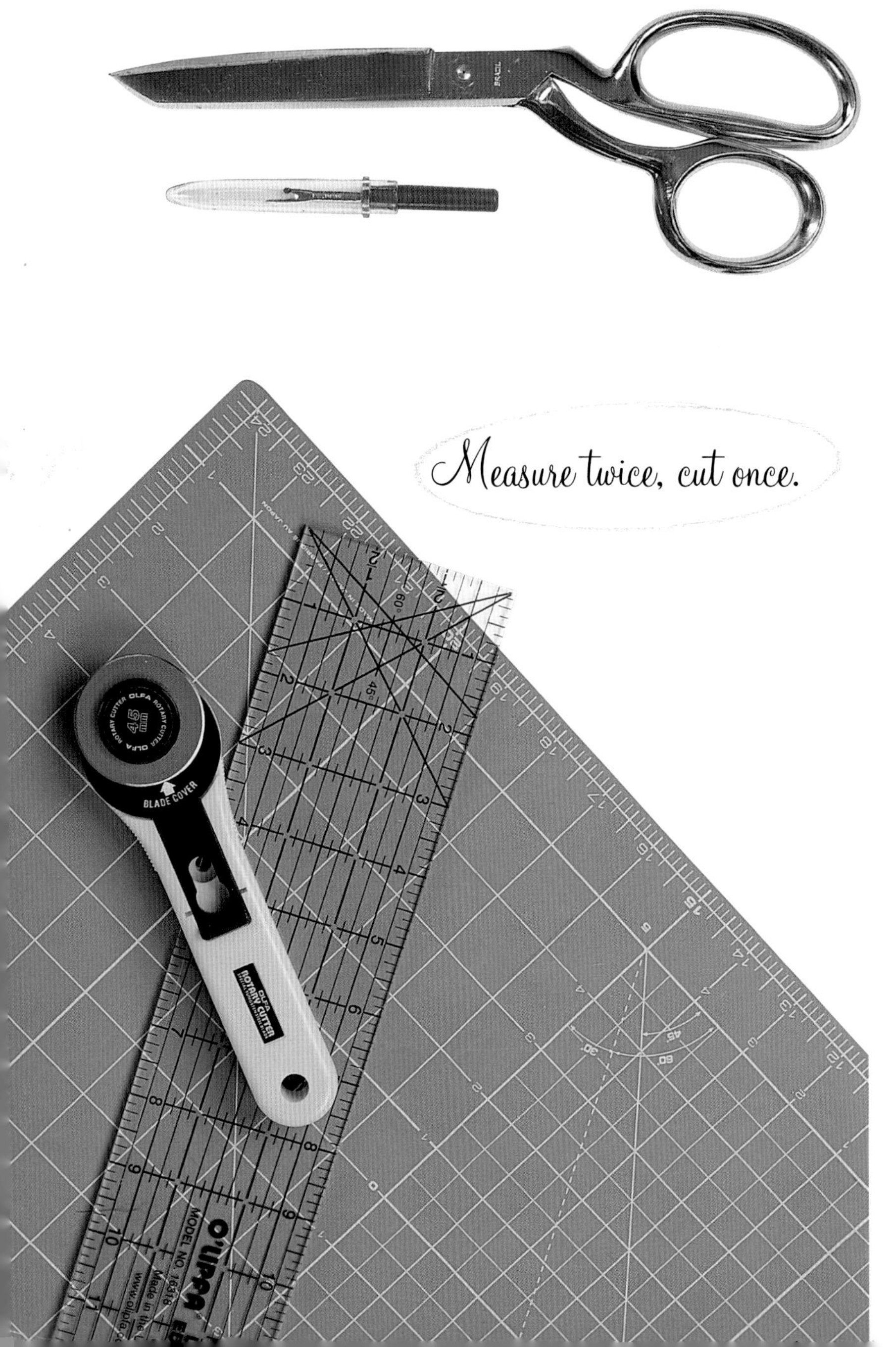

Measure twice, cut once.

SCISSORS. If you invest in only one quality item for making window treatments, I suggest a good pair of 7- or 8-inch dressmaker's bent-handled shears. The design of bent-handled shears allows the fabric to remain flat, so it doesn't shift while you're cutting. A pair of sewing scissors, say 4 to 5 inches long, is perfect for other cutting tasks, such as trimming seams. Buy the best pair of scissors you can afford, because you'll be friends forever. I still use my grandmother's sewing scissors, which are at least 30 (if not 40) years old.

A pair of pinking shears is handy for finishing seams. They're cute, too. But they shouldn't be used to cut out your curtain pieces.

ROTARY CUTTER. When you're cutting simple shapes, the rotary cutter is fast, efficient, and fun. We've used a rotary cutter on many of the projects in this book.

SEAM RIPPER. Change is inevitable, and so are mistakes. Use a seam ripper to remove stitches that displease you.

MEASURING TOOLS. If the only measuring tool you had were a tape measure, you could certainly make a curtain. But because measuring is so very important (remember you have to measure the window before you buy the fabric), you should also have a locking metal tape measure, too.

We can thank quilters for their cutting mats and clear rulers. Used in concert with a rotary cutter, these three tools make measuring and cutting a breeze, especially if you invest in one of the very large cutting mats. (They're also very helpful when straightening fabric, which we'll talk about on pages 28 and 29.) A sewing gauge is a nifty little tool that has a slider for marking lengths, and you may find it helpful when placing trim, tabs, or ties, for instance.

PINS AND NEEDLES. Basic dressmaker's pins will be fine for your early projects. Later on, you may want to add thin silk pins or long quilter's pins (with perky colorful heads) to your stash of sewing supplies. Quilter's pins can be quite useful when you're working with several layers of fabric, as you might do when you're making a mitered corner, for instance.

You'll do very simple hand sewing for some the projects in this book. An assortment of sharps (all-purpose sewing needles) will be just fine.

PINCUSHION. Store all of your pins and needles in a pincushion. You can get the ubiquitous tomato or the groovy felt orb, or perhaps try a magnetic pincushion. Lately I've come to favor the magnetic ones because they can grab the pins that have misbehaved and escaped to the floor.

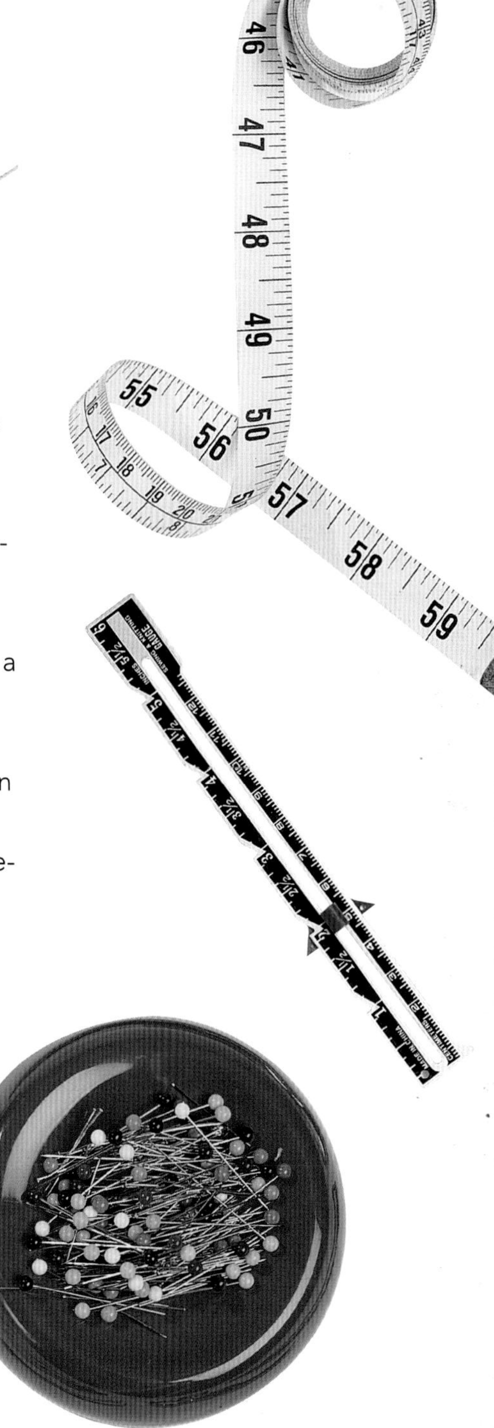

THREAD. All-purpose thread, which is cotton-wrapped polyester, is fine for any of the curtains in this book. As your adventure in sewing continues, you may eventually want to use all-cotton thread (great for woven, natural fiber fabrics) or perhaps all-polyester thread (good for fiber blends and knits). When you're choosing a thread color for your project, either match it to the fabric or choose a shade that's slightly darker.

MARKING TOOLS. Unlike garment sewing, where you have to mark lots of darts and circles and so on, you'll need to make only a few markings on your curtains, if any at all. Occasionally, you'll need to mark a tab or tie placement or something or the other. There are a couple of different ways you can accomplish this: with tailor's chalk or a chalk pencil, or with a water-soluble or air-soluble (i.e. disappearing) fabric pen. You should always test your markers on a scrap of your fabric to make sure they perform as advertised.

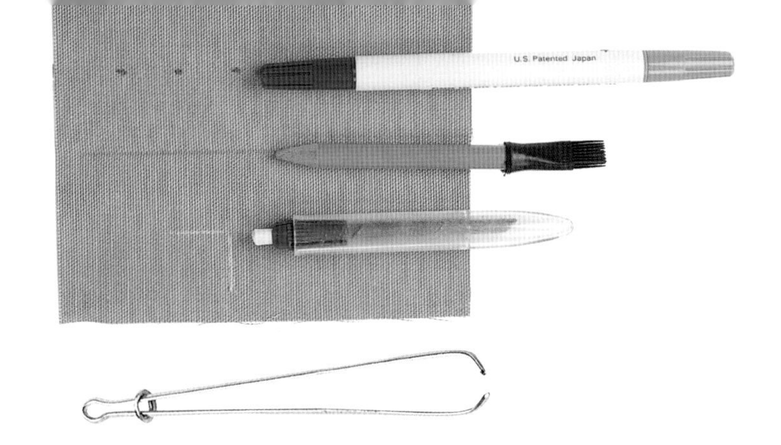

MISCELLANEOUS NOTIONS. In case you're interested (and I'm sure you are), notions include all the other things you need to sew besides the fabric. We've already talked about the most important things you'll need, but here's a quick word about a few other items.

We used *interfacing* in a couple of projects; interfacing is special fabric that's used to stabilize parts of your curtains. The interfacing used in this book is fusible, which means that it bonds to the fabric with heat and pressure. We also used paper-backed fusible web for making appliqués. This material bonds on both sides and is also set with heat. We used a little tool called a bodkin to make ties—it helps turn skinny things inside out.

DECORATIVE ELEMENTS. Ribbon, lace, buttons, beads, embroidery, appliqués, fringe, tassels—we've got it all. Read all about decorative techniques on page 47.

IRON. An iron is a very important tool in all types of sewing. When making window treatments, you'll do lots of pressing of hems, for example.

Note that we're not talking about *ironing,* which is sliding your iron across the fabric. We're talking about *pressing.* Pressing is moving the iron across the fabric in increments by pressing it up and down. If you can, press open each seam as you sew, before it's overlapped or crossed by another seam.

We're almost ready to start sewing.
Grab a cup of java.

Learn to Sew!

In all honesty, a curtain is just about the easiest sewing project you can imagine. We're going to cut the fabric; mark the pieces, if we need to; and stitch it up. That's it! Sewing is really a lot like the process of cooking: you choose a recipe (the curtain style); buy the ingredients (fabric and notions); do the washing and chopping (preparing and cutting out the fabric); then add the ingredients to one another according to the recipe (sew by following the project instructions). See—easy as pie. Or, if you'd rather—a piece of cake.

Let's get started by readying our fabric.

Prepare the fabric

You have to know a little more about fabric to understand the importance of the proper layout and subsequent cutting of your window treatment, so bear with me a moment. When we discussed fabric earlier, we talked about prewashing. Now, prewashing actually means *shrinking,* as many washable fabrics will do just that when laundered. Generally, the looser the weave, the more shrinkage is likely to occur. Washing also removes sizing or finishes that may affect the quality of your stitches. Check the label on the bolt of cloth for the laundering recommendations, and launder the fabric the same way you plan to launder your curtain. Please don't neglect this very important step, because you'll be totally bummed to wash your curtain for the first time and then find that it's become too small for its window! After you've laundered your fabric, press it to remove any wrinkles. (Remember: press, not iron.)

Align the grain

Your fabric must be correctly aligned before you cut out the curtain pieces, and here's why. (We'll get to the how in just a few minutes.) Woven fabric is made of lengthwise and crosswise threads. In a perfect world, the crosswise threads are perpendicular to the lengthwise threads. The direction of these threads is called the *grain.*

Your curtain pieces must follow the proper direction of the grain, or they won't hang properly. Most garment pieces follow the lengthwise (or straight) grain, because the lengthwise threads are designed to be stronger to withstand the tension of the weaving process. Curtains almost always have to be cut along this lengthwise grain because the width is finite (45 inches, 54 inches, etc.), while the length is not. Generally, you don't see curtains with seams bisecting the length, as you want a continuous flow of fabric along the drop.

You should also know about *bias;* the bias flows along the diagonal between the lengthwise and crosswise threads. This is the direction in which woven fabric has the most stretch. While we won't cut any fabric along the bias, file this fact away because it helps you understand why it's so important to cut the fabric properly—your curtain may stretch out of shape if it's not cut along the lengthwise grain.

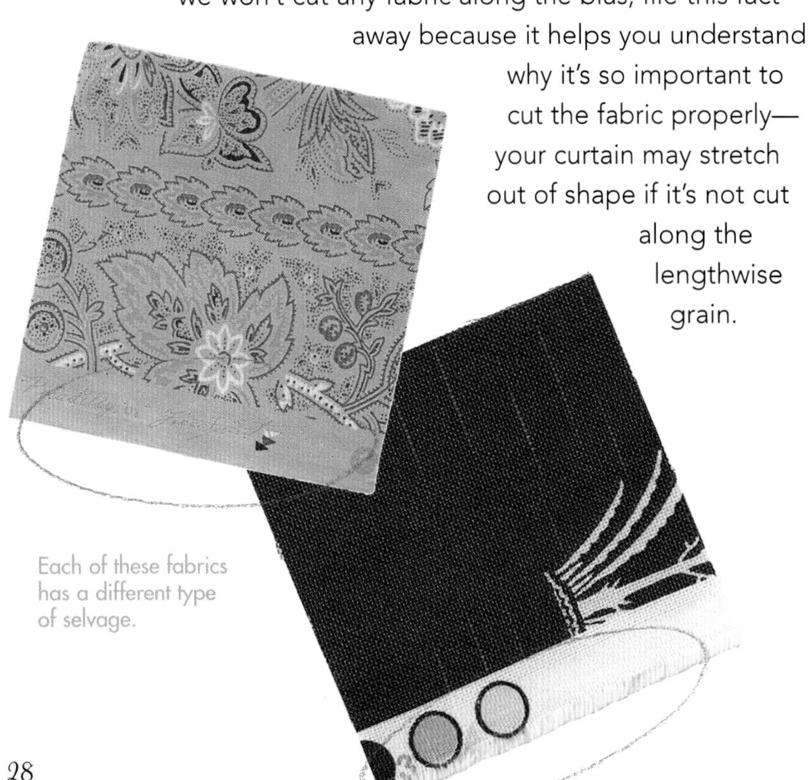

Each of these fabrics has a different type of selvage.

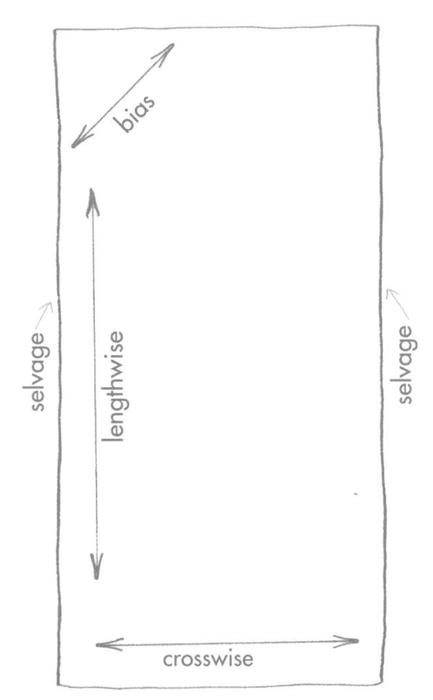

Here's how the grain flows in a length of fabric.

When making almost anything else *except* a window treatment, you would fold the fabric before you cut out the pieces. But with a curtain, you're generally using the entire width for one panel, so you should place the entire piece, unfolded, on a flat surface. Smooth out the fabric so it's flat. To align the grain, you'll square the fabric edges, working from the finished border on the length of the fabric, which is the *selvage.* This border differs in appearance from fabric to fabric, but you'll be able to recognize it.

FIGURE 4

There are several ways to square the edges. One is to clip into the selvage and pull out a crosswise thread across the entire width of the fabric. Then, trim the edge evenly along this visible line, as you see in figure 4. After you've trimmed away the excess fabric, the cut end and the selvages should be perpendicular to one another.

If your fabric seems too thick to pull out a thread (and some decorator fabrics are), here are a couple of other ways to straighten the grain. Use a cutting mat and clear ruler to straighten the crosswise edges or, as in figure 5, do the same thing with a carpenter's square (one of those shiny L-shaped rulers that your significant other may have in the workshop). If you're using fabric with a motif that follows the crosswise grain across the fabric, you can also cut along this design (figure 6).

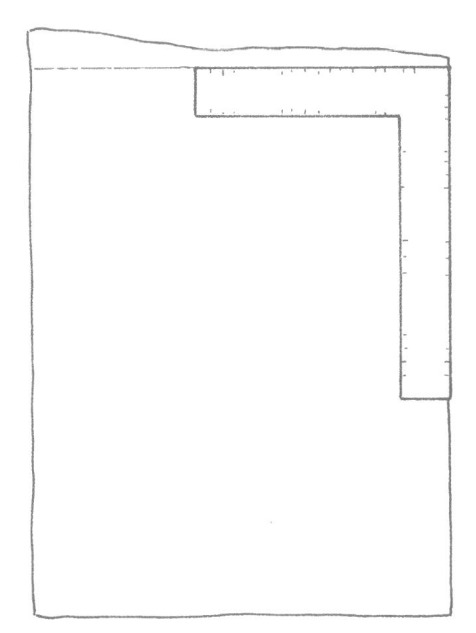
FIGURE 5

FIGURE 6

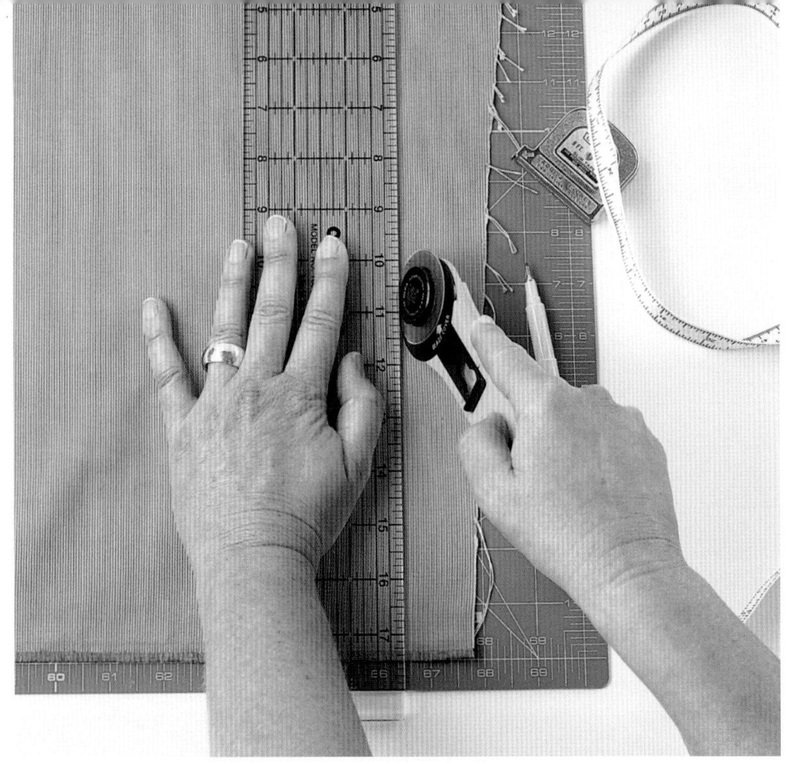

Cutting the fabric to the proper length

Aligning with the straight grain

Cut out the curtain pieces

Since you're all smart enough to make your own window treatments, you've probably figured out that you need a lot of space to cut out your curtain panels. And you'd be absolutely correct. A large table, or a nice clean floor, will do nicely if you're thrifty; if you'd like to invest in your sewing future, buy an extra-large cutting mat.

After squaring the fabric, use your measurements to cut each panel, marking the dimensions with a fabric pen, pencil, or chalk. (If your fabric is wider than your panel will be, you may need to cut away some of the width, too. If your finished panel needs to be wider than your fabric, remember to add an inch to the finished width for each seam). Follow your markings as you cut, using shears or a rotary cutter. Mark the top of each panel. Trim away the selvages.

Remember when we talked about the grain of the fabric? One of our projects (Stylish Swag, on page 82) has pieces that need to be aligned with the straight grain of the fabric when you cut them out. On the pattern pieces you'll see a line with arrows at either end; place the pieces on the fabric, with the line following the lengthwise grain. Measure from each arrow until they're the same distance from the selvage; keep tweaking until they're equidistant and the line is parallel with the selvage. Pin in place and cut.

Finally!
We're ready to sew.

Start to sew

Okay, let's go! I hope you're as excited as I am. We've chosen a curtain style, purchased the fabric and notions, and cut out the pieces. Read through the next section and promise me you'll sit down at the sewing machine and practice stitching before you get started. Remember to familiarize yourself with your sewing machine and its controls (Did I already tell you this?), and set up your workspace so all your tools and materials are handy.

In the following section, we'll talk about the basic techniques that we've used in our curtain projects. Don't try to remember everything at once, but read it through so you have a general understanding of the process. Later, in the Make a Curtain! section, you'll see how the techniques work in context when you make your own curtain. We've presented them here with contrasting stitching so you can easily see what happens during each step. Furthermore, we've used fabric that's similar to what we used for many of our curtains (cotton), so you can see real-world examples of how these fabrics behave when they're sewn. This isn't computer-enhanced sewing we're doing here.

Hemming the edges of the Sarong Curtain (page 54)

And you may notice real-world sewing in your projects, too—fabrics fray when they're handled and some techniques (like gathering) put more stress on the fabric, so you'll probably see a thread or two. Do tidy up when you're done, trimming all the loose threads. Remember, this isn't work—it's fun and you're just beginning. So plug in the machine, turn on the lights, and let's sew. If you need a refresher course when you're making your curtain, you can always flip back to these illustrated techniques.

Our 3 helpful stitches

Stitch a seam

To avoid boggling your mind, we've kept the sewing fairly simple in *Fun & Fabulous Curtains*, using only basic techniques. There are three stitches: the straight stitch, the basting stitch, and the zigzag. The straight stitch is the foundation of your curtain; you can also do the straight stitch in reverse to anchor the beginning of your seams or to provide reinforcement at certain points, such as the end of a line of trim. (Consult our friend the manual for reverse stitching.) The basting stitch is simply a straight stitch set to a longer length. Use basting stitches to hold layers together temporarily or to gather fabric. Zigzag stitches are used to finish the raw edges of seams, or for just plain fun.

When you're practicing, use a contrasting thread so you can easily see what's happening. Also, use two pieces of fabric for the best results; sewing machines are designed to join two layers of fabric, so the top and bobbin stitches meet in the middle. Refer to You Know What for the proper way to thread your machine, wind the bobbin, and accurately set the stitch length. A setting of 10–12 stitches per inch is average for the type of sewing we're doing.

To sew a seam, align the fabric edges and pin them together with the pins perpendicular, with the heads near the edge. Line up the fabric to the ½-inch guideline on your

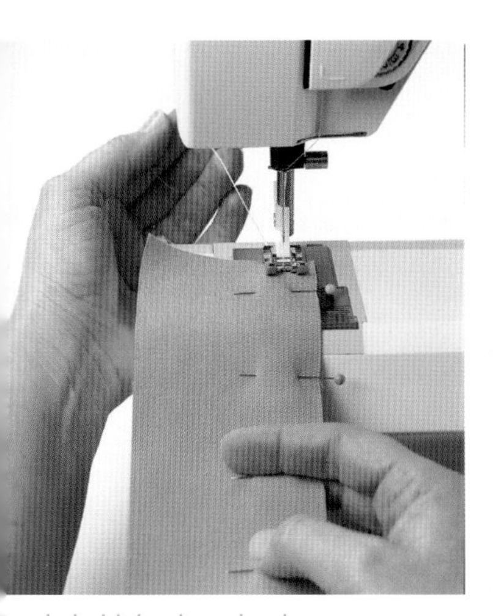

ently hold the threads when
ou begin stitching.

ewing machine's needle plate; ½-inch seam allowances are tandard in home décor sewing. lace the fabric underneath the eedle just a tiny bit (oh, ¼ inch) way from the end of the fabric. ower the presser foot. (Do emember to do this because narly things happen if you forget.) Hold the bobbin and top hreads while you backstitch a ouple of stitches to the end of he seam. Let go of the threads nd stitch forward, pausing to emove the pins as you go. Don't, don't, *don't* be tempted o stitch over the pins—you can reak a needle, or worse, ruin our machine's timing by hitting pin. Or even worse, have hards of metal flying around ou and your curtain.

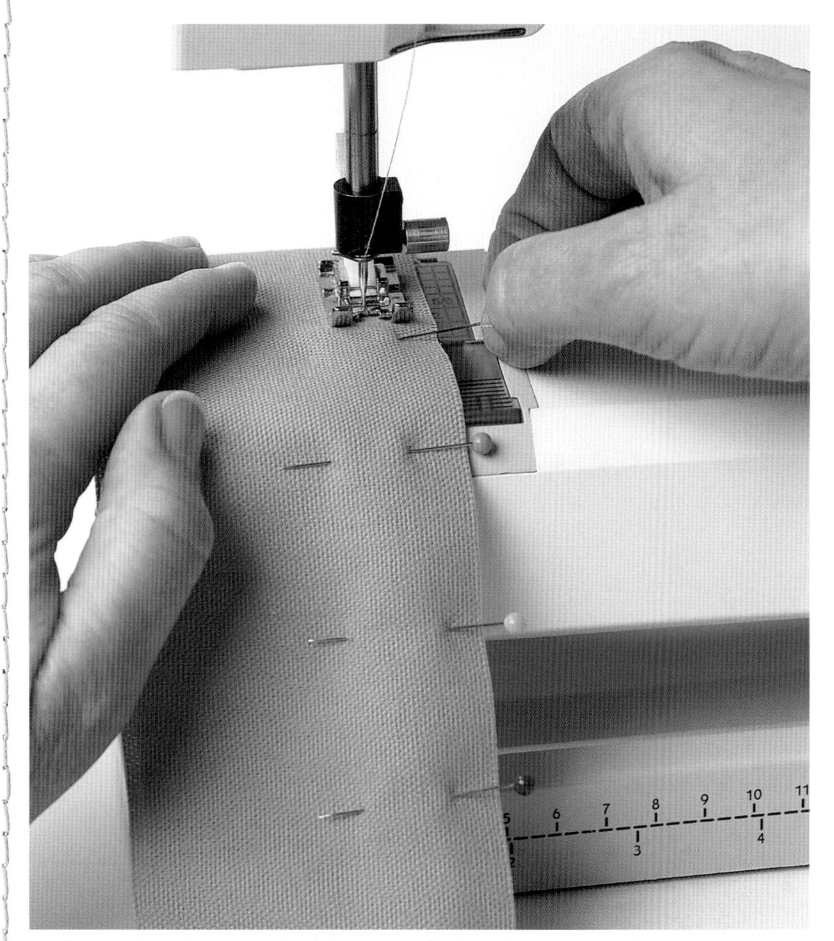

Let the machine do the work while you guide the fabric. Remove the pins before you reach them.

Guide the fabric lightly with your hands, keeping it straight against the guideline on your needle plate. Watch the guideline and not the needle—it can be hypnotizing. (Really!) Let the machine do the work of pulling the fabric along (that's what those busy little feed dogs do). When you reach the end of the seam, backstitch for a few stitches to secure.

Congratulations—you've just stitched your first seam. Go get a latte.

Balance the tension

After your coffee (and maybe a snack too), take a moment to admire your first seam. Look at both sides of the fabric; the stitches should look nearly identical on each side, being locked between the two pieces of fabric. If they don't look identical, you may need to adjust the thread tension on your machine. Each thread (top and bobbin) has its own tension. You may need to make adjustments to the tension according to the type of fabric you're using to make your curtain. Every time you sew with a new fabric, you should check the tension first.

The examples at the right show correct tension; top tension that's too tight; and top tension that's too loose. When the top tension is too tight, it yanks the poor bobbin thread up to the right side of the fabric; the opposite happens when the top tension is too loose. Following the instructions in (guess what?) your manual, make small adjustments at a time and do test seams until you're happy with the tension setting.

To check thread tension, use different colors of the same type of thread—one color (pink) on top, the other (white) in the bobbin.

The example above shows correct tension.

Here, the top tension is too tight.

This example shows top tension that's too loose.

Pivot

When you're sewing, you occasionally have to change direction—just like driving. When you need to do an about-face, you do so like this: stop with the needle in the fabric. Raise your presser foot and turn the fabric. Lower your presser foot and have at it!

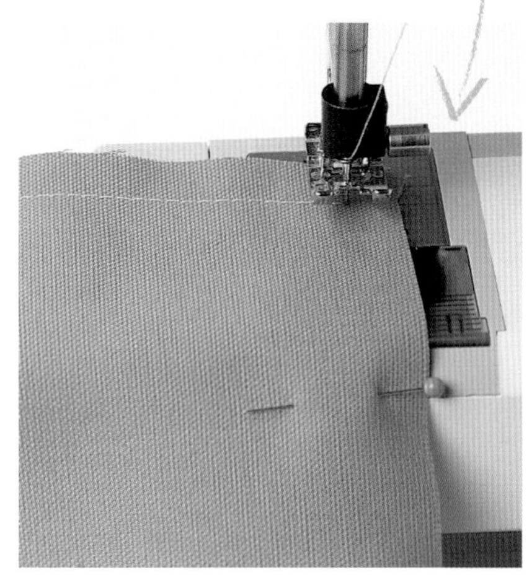

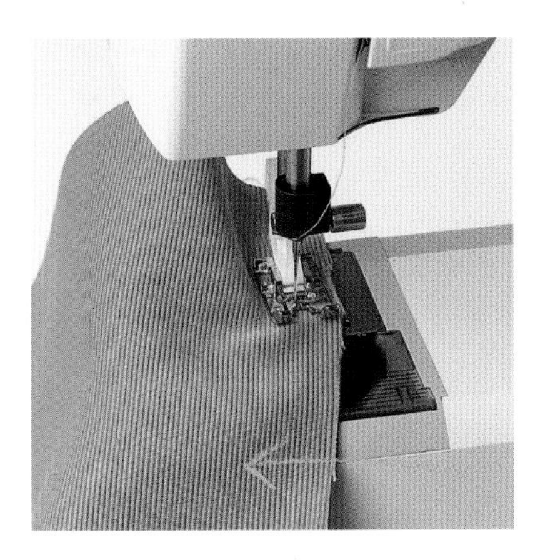

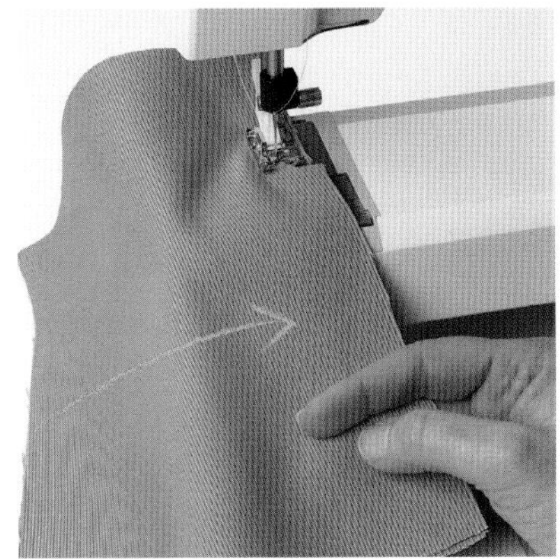

Guide the fabric

Sometimes you don't need a complete change of direction, just some friendly guidance. Use a gentle pull of the fabric to keep the fabric aligned on your needle plate.

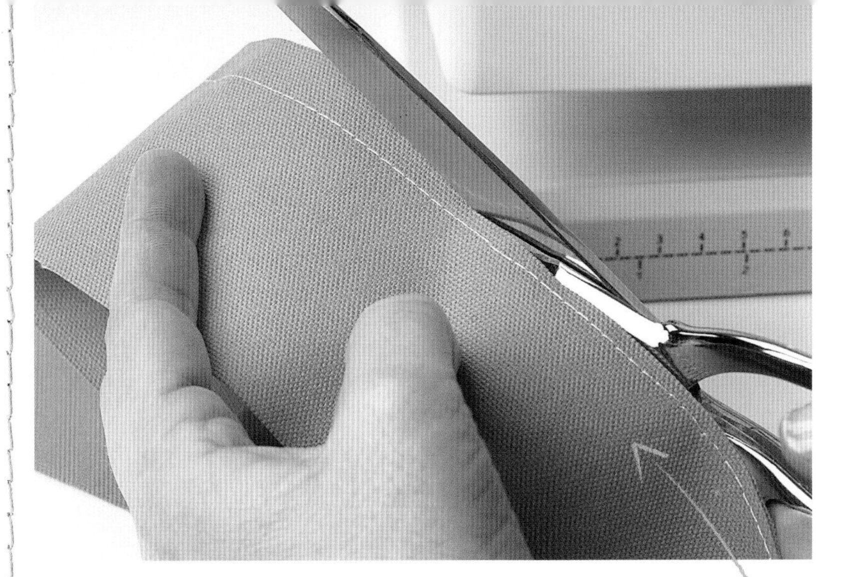

Trim seams and clip curves

When you sew, you occasionally need to trim a seam, especially if you're using bulky fabric. Our project instructions will tell you when to do this. Generally, you trim a seam to reduce bulk in the finished curtain. Simply use your shears to trim away the seam allowance to about ¼ inch.

Curved seams demand a little extra attention. If you have any curved seams, you'll need to notch the curves every inch or so to allow the seams to lie flat. Cut notches in the seam allowance to eliminate fullness, using just the tips of the scissors, or use your pinking shears for quickie notching.

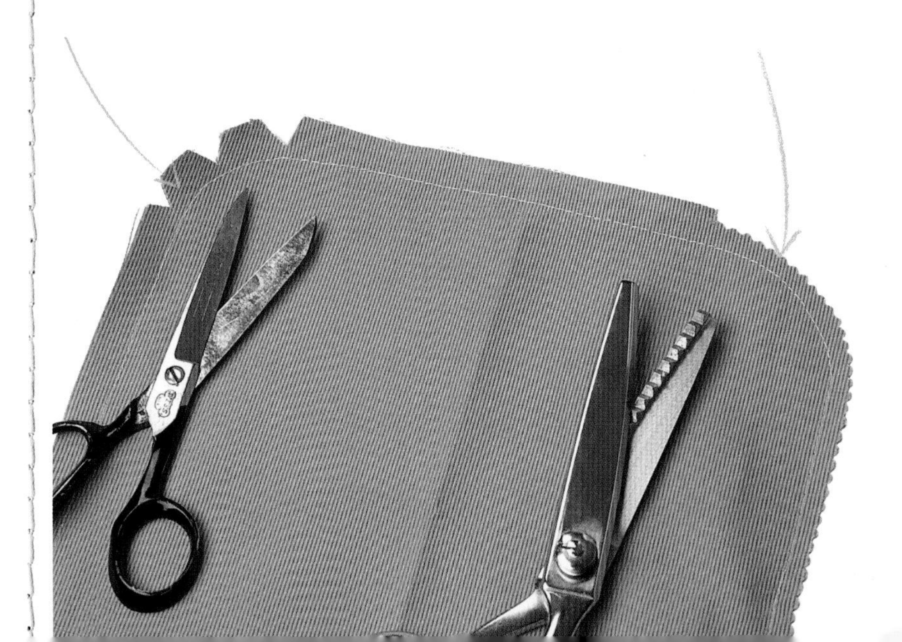

Finish the seams

Conventional sewing wisdom says that all exposed seams should be finished in some manner, to prevent raveling and increase the longevity of your project. Sounds like good advice to me. Because of the construction of many of our projects, most of our raw edges are covered (unless we left them on display on purpose). So we have very few seams that require finishing. But here are a few simple methods we used every once in a while.

ZIGZAG. If you want to finish the seams before you sew, sew a line of zigzag stitching into the seam allowance, as close to the cut edge as you can. This is a good choice for fabrics that tend to ravel easily. After stitching the seam, press it open. If you're using a lightweight fabric, you might find that it's a little tricky to stitch into the single thickness without the fabric puckering, so use one of the methods that follow instead.

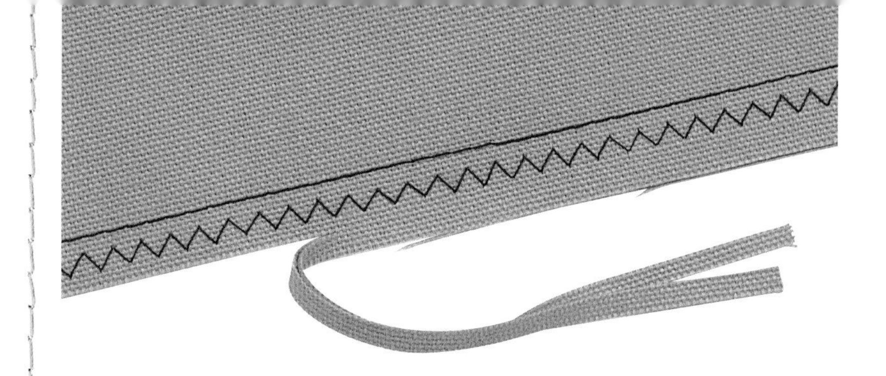

DOUBLE-STITCHED. The double-stitched seam is good for extra stability. After the seam has been sewn, stitch a parallel line of stitching in the seam allowance, then trim away close to the second line of stitching. Press to one side. (You could do a second line of stitching in a frisky little zigzag, too.)

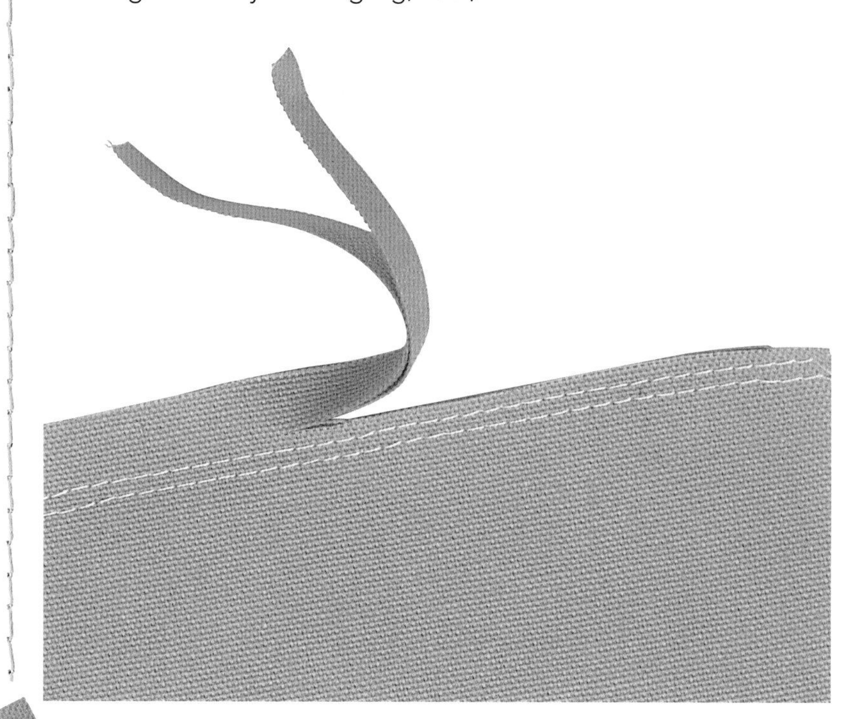

PINKED. This is a good choice for tightly woven fabrics. After stitching the seam, trim with pinking shears. Press open to finish.

FRENCH SEAM. This is an enclosed seam that's perfect for sheer fabrics, and perfect for curtains, because all the raw edges are enclosed. Begin by stitching the *wrong* sides together in a 1/4-inch seam. Trim the seam to within a millimeter of its life (that is, very short) and turn the fabric inside out so the right sides are together. Now, stitch together in a 1/4-inch seam, encasing the raw edge. You've created a traditional-looking seam on the outside and a neat fold on the inside. You can use this method on straight seams only.

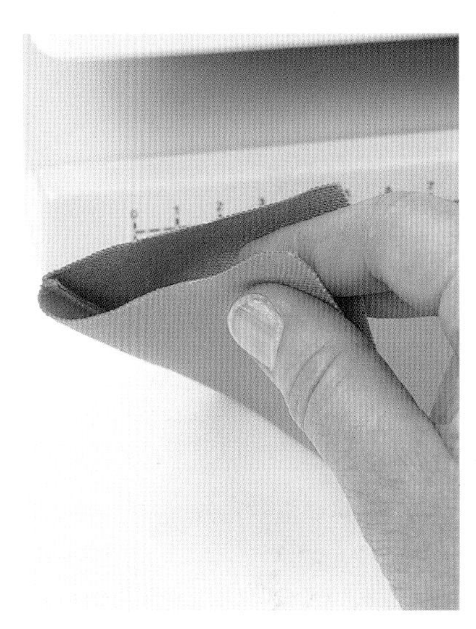

Right sides together

You'll almost always sew the pieces of your curtain with the right sides together (facing each other). This is the most basic fact you need to remember about sewing in general. If your fabric doesn't have easily recognizable right and wrong sides, you'll have to decide which is which. Then be sure to mark each piece.

Make a narrow hem

Several of the curtains in this book have edges that are finished with narrow hems. It's just like it sounds: a skinny little hem that's stitched in place on the machine. Typically they're made like this: Stitch 1/2 inch or so from the raw edge and press up along this line of stitching. Tuck under the raw edge to meet the stitching, forming a nice fold. Press and stitch in place along the fold.

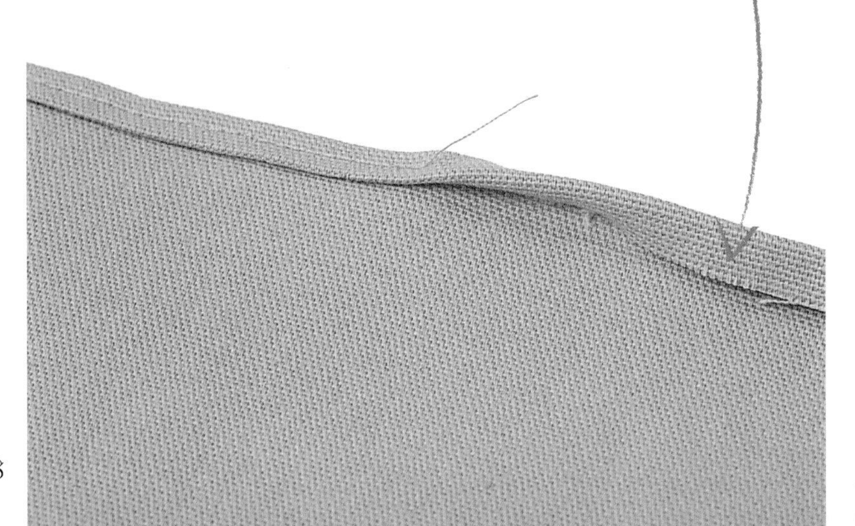

Now, there's also a *very* narrow hem, which is great for sheer or lightweight fabrics. To make a very narrow hem, machine-stitch 3/8 inch from the raw edge. Turn under on the line of stitching and stitch close to fold. Trim the fabric close to the stitching line. Turn under 1/8 inch, encasing the raw edge. Stitch the hem in place. Press.

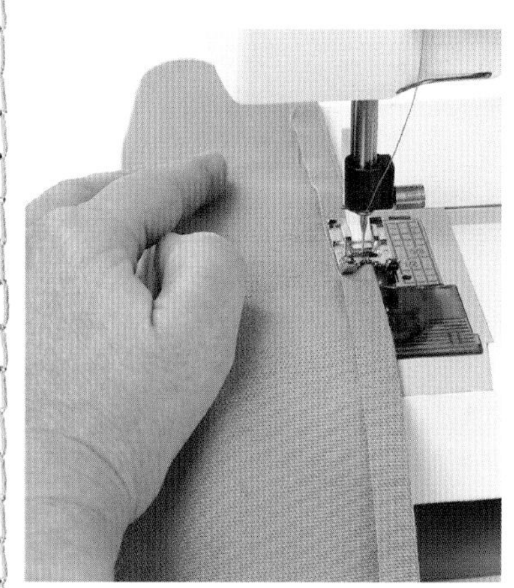

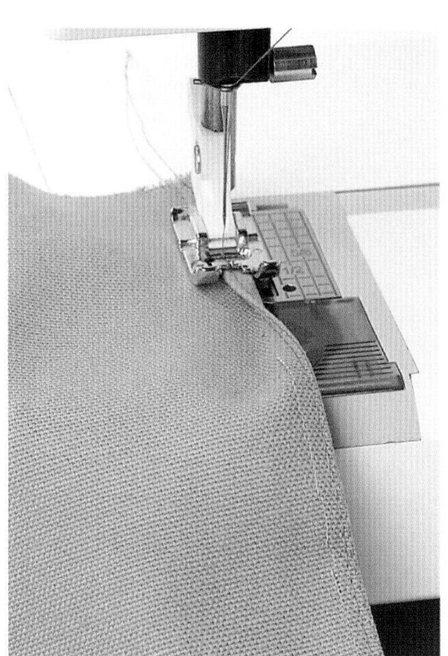

Make a double hem

Most simple curtains (the kind this book is all about) are hemmed at the sides and the bottom. Standard practice is to use a *double hem* (also known as a double-fold hem). Double hems provide stability and add weight to the edges of your window treatments.

You can probably guess what a double hem is: two equal-sized folds that are stitched down. The most accurate way to do this is to first fold the complete depth of the hem, let's say 4 inches. Press the fold. Now, turn under the raw edge to meet the pressed fold, which leaves a 2-inch hem. Press again, and stitch in place. The fold we just described would be referred to as a 2-inch double hem.

Add a heading

As we talked about before, there are many ways to construct the top of your curtain. If you were planning just a basic curtain—a rectangle hemmed on all four sides—you could simply hang it with clip rings and be done with it. But you might want more from your curtain—and you shall have it!

ROD POCKET. This easy heading, also called a casing, or maybe even a channel, is formed by a couple of simple folds. Turn under 2½ to 5 inches (depending on the diameter of your curtain rod) and press. Turn under ½ inch on the raw edge and press. Pin and stitch in place.

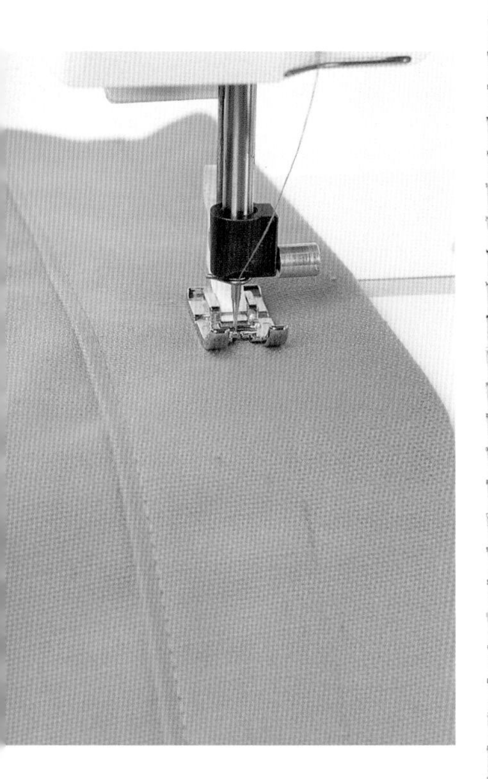

ROD POCKET WITH HEADER. This header is made from extra fabric that forms a flourish at the top of the curtain. To construct it, you'll add one more row of stitching between the top of the curtain and the rod, forming an inner casing, so you must factor in the extra fabric. Add twice the depth of the header to the amount you allow for the casing. (For instance, if you allowed 4 inches for your casing and wanted a 2-inch header, you would add another 4 inches for the header, allowing 8 inches for the header and casing combined.) For the best fit, your lines of stitching should snugly encase the rod.

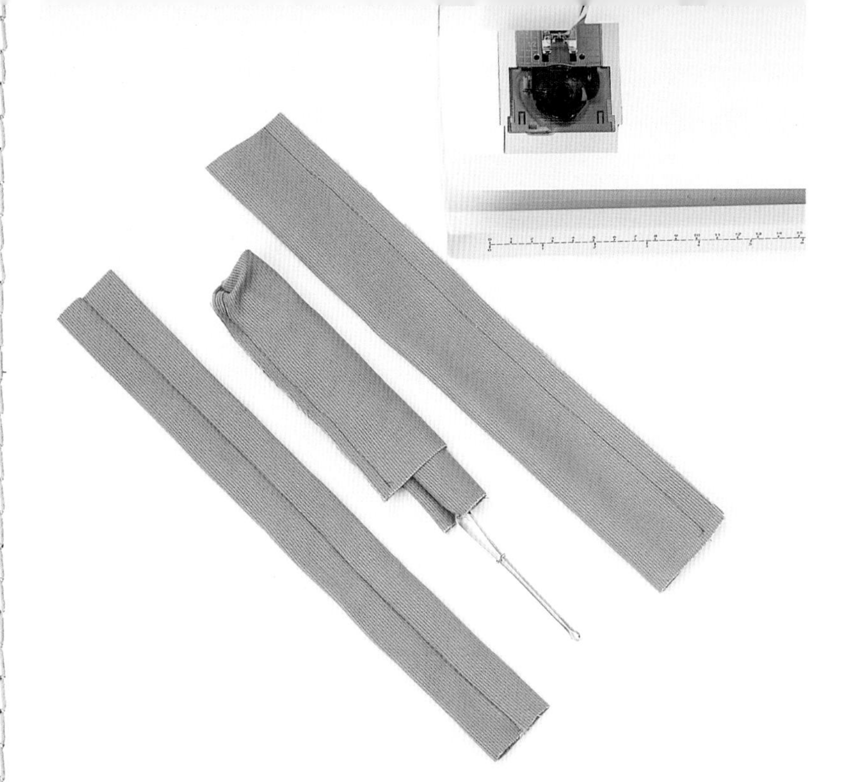

TABS. This heading style really suits casual curtains, yet can be used for sophisticated silk or linen curtains, too. Tabs offer a great opportunity to show off a decorative curtain rod, as much of it will be visible through the tabs.

Tabs can be as narrow as an inch, or as wide as several inches, depending upon your preference. To determine the length of your tabs, wrap a scrap of fabric around your curtain rod and mark your desired size. Add an inch for seam allowances and double your desired width, again adding an inch for seam allowances. Cut as many tabs as needed; they should be spaced from 6 to 8 inches along the top of your curtain.

To make the tab, you'll place the right sides together and fold the piece in half along its length. Stitch in a 1/2-inch seam. Turn the tab right side out and place the seam in the center of the back of the tab. Press.

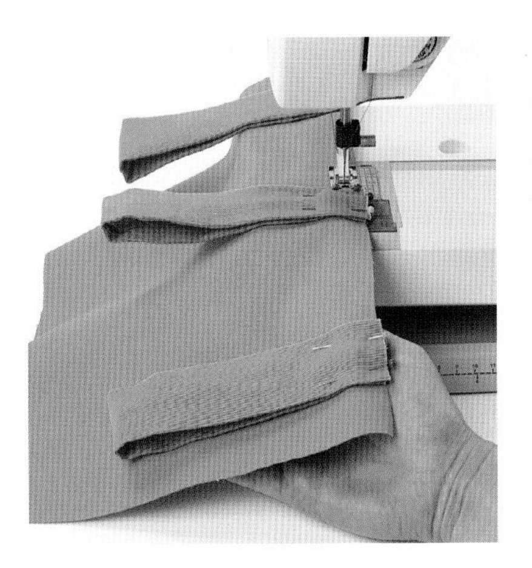

Tabs are usually basted to the window treatment and stitched in place between the curtain and a *facing*, an extra piece of fabric that's cut to the width of the curtain. Look to the individual project instructions for specifics on adding tabs.

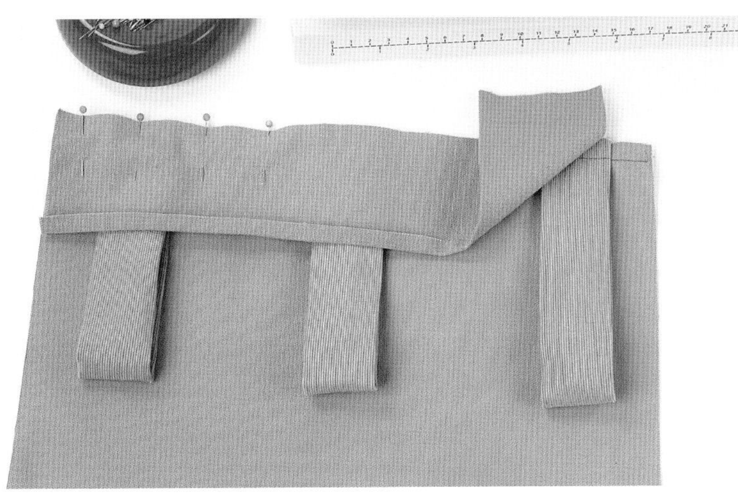

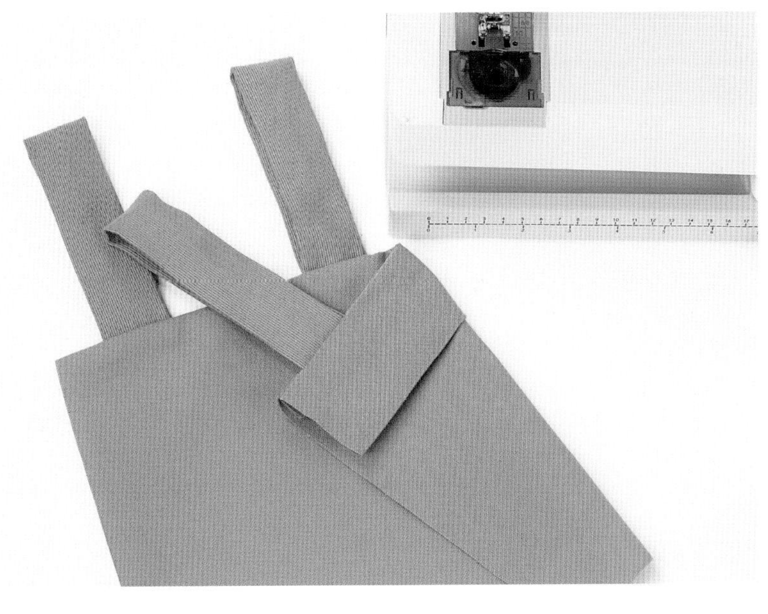

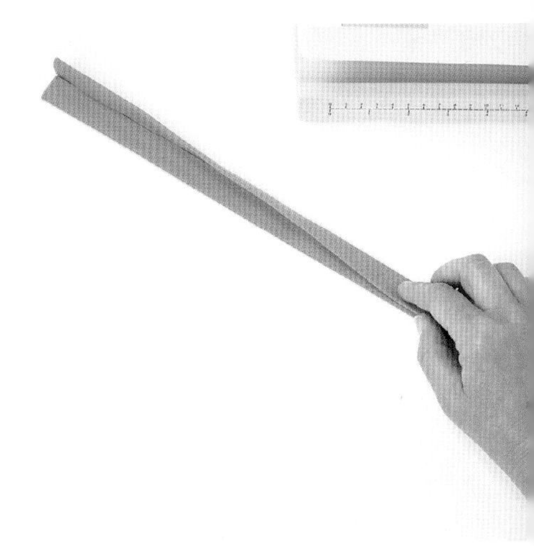

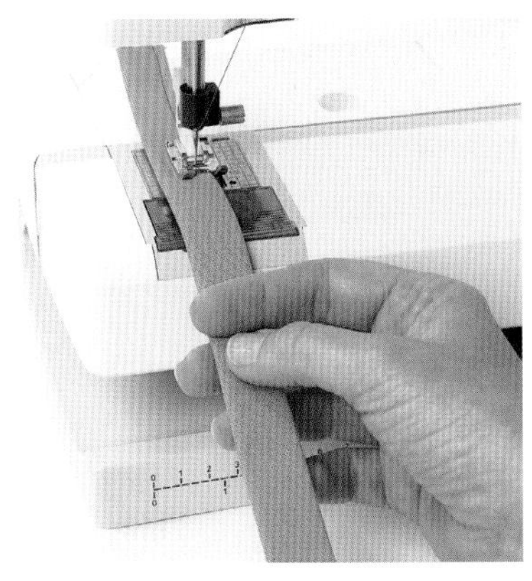

TIES. There are a couple of ways you can make ties for your curtains. The easiest tie is created like so: cut a piece of fabric to the length you want the tie. Fold it in half lengthwise and press; turn each raw edge into the center and press again. Stitch. Knot the ends. Stitch to the curtain according to the project instructions.

Hint—
you can also use ribbon for a ready-made tie.

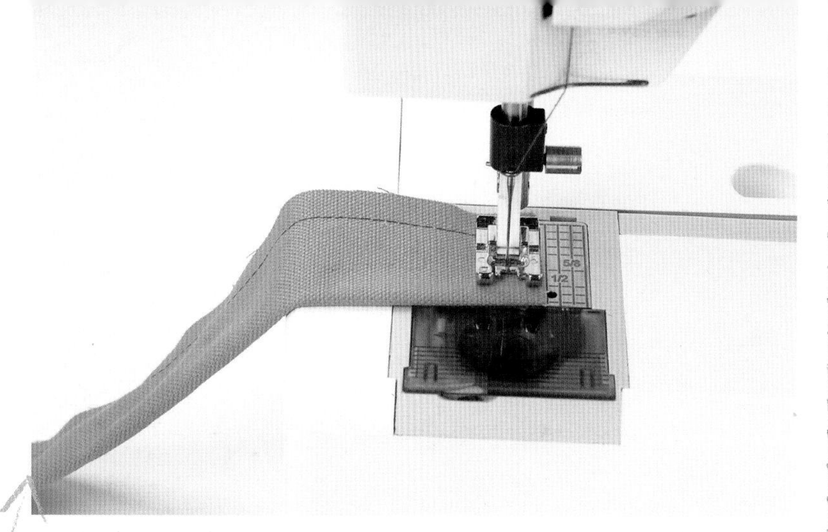

Making a skinny tube tie is slightly more involved, but not much. Here are two methods. For the first, stitch a length of fabric together with the right sides facing and—presto!—turn it inside out. Because these ties are narrow, you'll need some way to turn them inside out. There are several gadgets you can buy to turn tubes, or you can just attach a safety pin to one end and thread the pin back through the tube, pulling it right side out.

For the second method, fold the fabric with right sides together and stitch along the length, pivot, and stitch across the end. Use an object like a pencil to push against the seam on the end, turning the tube inside out.

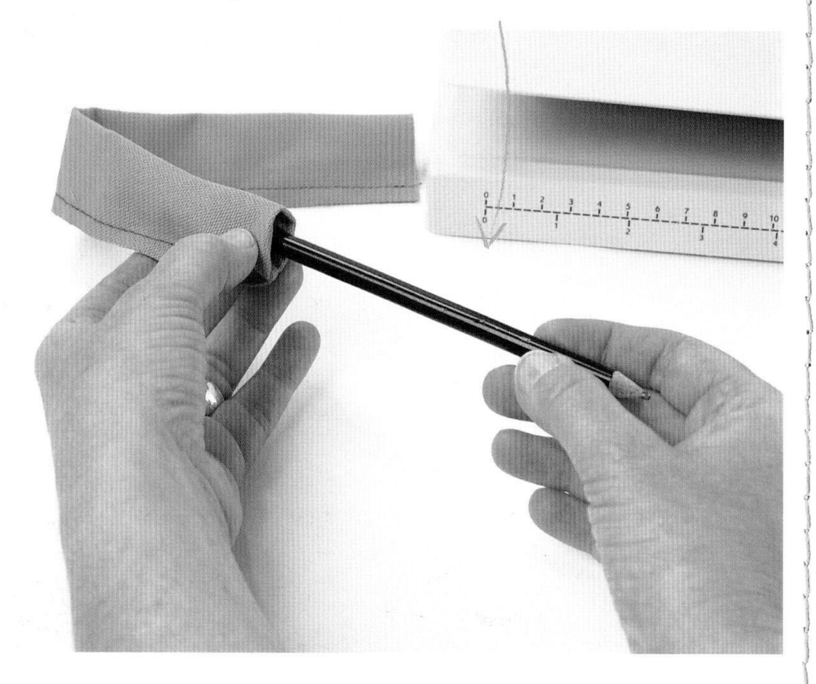

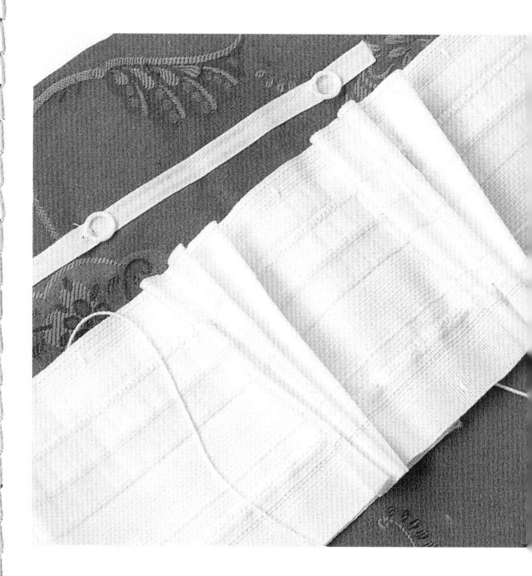

GROMMETS AND HEADER TAPES. You'll also see a couple of projects in *Fun & Fabulous Curtains* that employ these nifty things to make curtain headings. Although we give some general advice in the project section, we're going to cop out and ask that you follow the manufacturer's instructions when you use these products, because each company's stuff is a little bit different. Ask for assistance at your fabric shop if you need some guidance about these items.

CLIP RINGS. If you use clip rings, all you have to do to the heading of your curtain is finish it with a double hem and you're ready to hang. A link ring is a variation of a clip ring; it has two interlocking rings instead of a clip. Often, these will be sewn into place.

Miter the edges

Occasionally, you'll hem all the way around a curtain, and you'll want to have some tidy corners. A mitered corner is one that's been folded to eliminate bulk and, well, just look good, too. This technique works when you're hemming an equal length on each side.

Press under your desired hem on each edge. Open out the folds. (If you've got a double hem, unfold one fold only.) Fold the corner diagonally at the spot where the two fold lines intersect; the previous fold lines should align (photo 1). Press across the corner fold. To check what you're doing, fold again along the original hemline. Your edges should meet in a perfect little angle. Unfold once more and trim away the excess corner (go ahead, do it!), leaving about ½ inch of fabric (photo 2). Fold back into the mitered edge (photo 3). Stitch in place (photo 4), slipstitching the mitered edges together if desired.

Photo 1

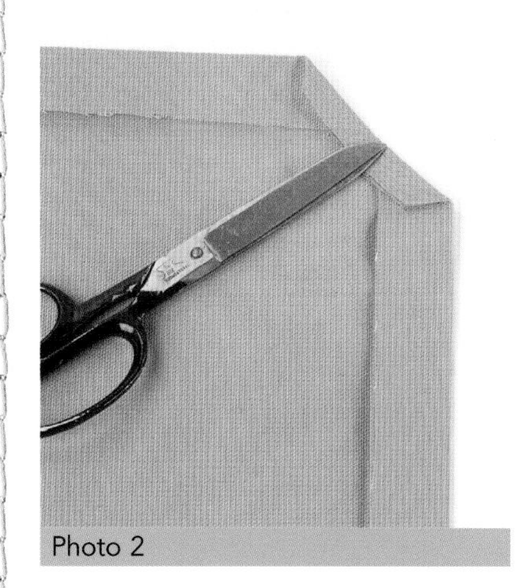

Photo 2

Photo 3

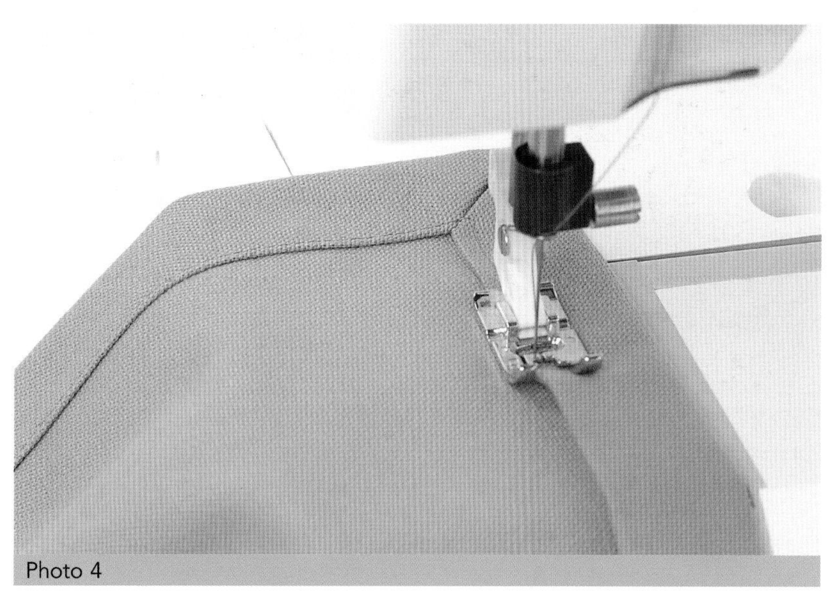

Photo 4

Add a facing

A facing is a piece of fabric used to finish an edge. In this book, facings are used to finish the heading of a curtain. They're usually cut to the length of the piece being finished and are several inches wide. We used a facing when we stitched on the tabs on page 41, remember?

Add a ruffle

Ruffles add a little bit of whimsy to anything. You can use ruffles to decorate the edge or hem of a curtain, and you can also use them as a simple decorative element. A ruffle is simply a long strip of fabric that is gathered to fit your curtain. A single ruffle is gathered along one long edge, while a double ruffle is gathered in the middle, between its two long edges. (In a fancy magazine, you may also see a double ruffle referred to as a *ruche*.)

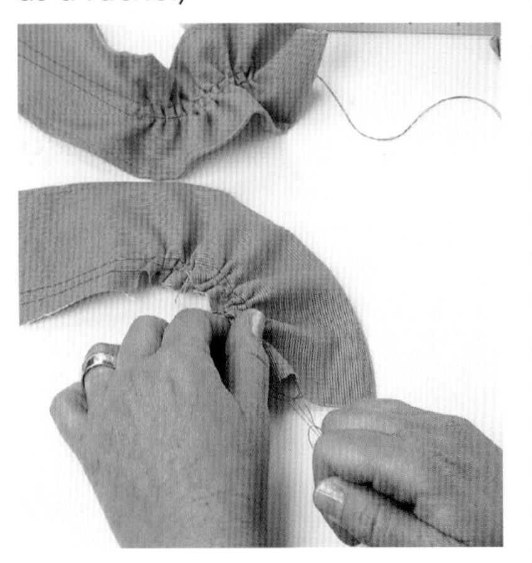

To make a single ruffle, make a narrow hem along one long edge. Gather the ruffle by making two rows of basting stitches along the remaining long edge; don't trim the thread ends. Pull the threads to gather the ruffles to the approximate length needed. Pin in place and adjust the gathers for balance. To make a double ruffle, follow the same procedure as just described, but finish both long edges and make the rows of basting stitches down the center of the fabric.

Add some pleats

If you're into the tailored look, try making some pleats in your curtain. Pleats are simply folds of fabric that are stitched into place. (You've got a skirt with pleats, I bet.) Pleats do require some yardage, though; simple 1-inch knife pleats, that all fold in the same direction, require 3 inches of fabric to make. Our project on page 98 describes how to estimate the yardage and make pleats. Basically, you mark foldlines, match the marks, and stitch.

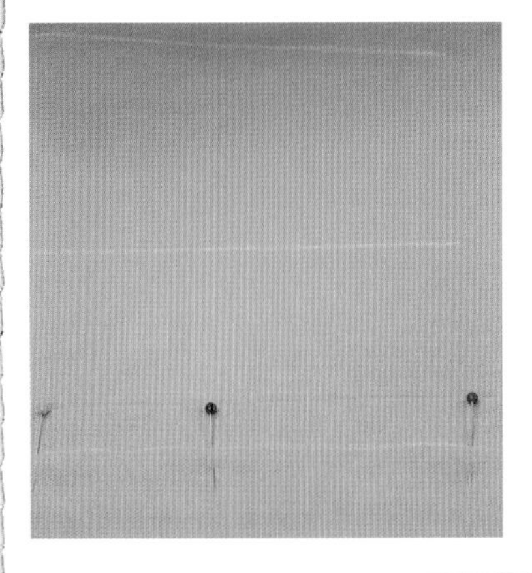

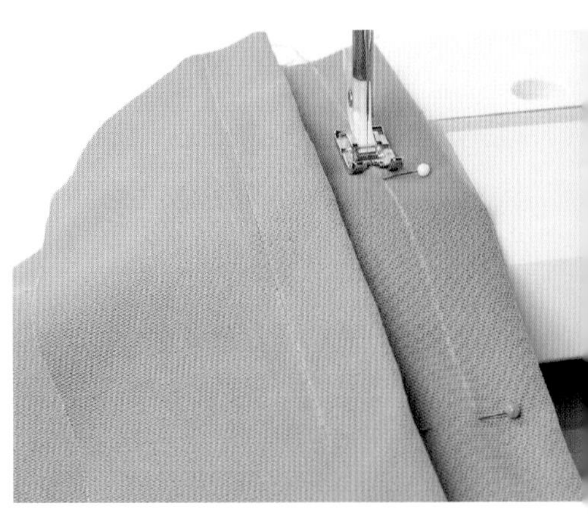

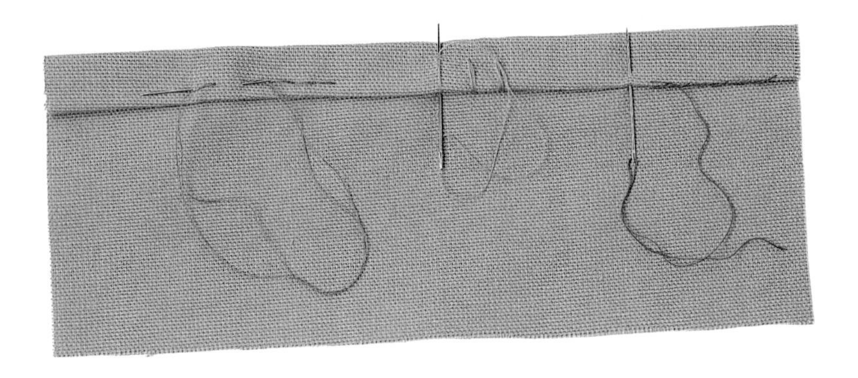

Hemstitches in pink thread, tacks in blue thread, and backstitches in orange thread

The projects are just ahead!

Stitch by hand

You need only a few basic hand stitches to make the curtains in this book. Begin all hand stitches with a knot in the thread.

One stitch you're likely to use is the hemstitch. A hemstitch is begun with the needle inserted into the fold of the fabric. Work from right to left as you pick up just a thread or two in the fabric and then insert the needle into the edge of the fold above the first stitch; the needle should be perpendicular to the fold. Repeat, making stitches every ¼ inch or so.

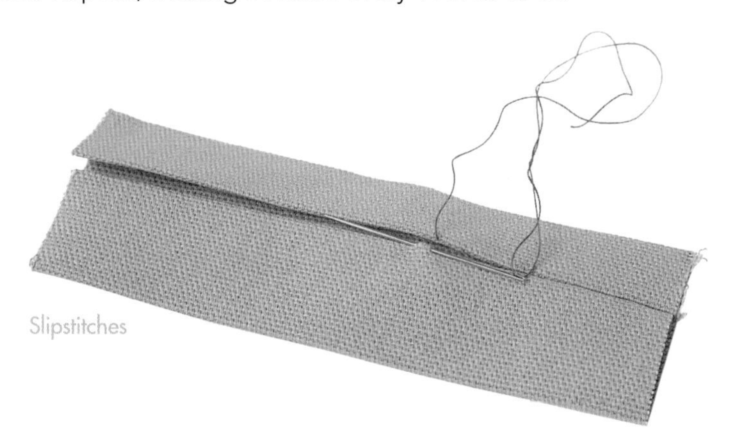

Slipstitches

Another stitch you may use is the slipstitch, a fairly invisible little stitch. A slipstitch is used between two folded edges, to secure a mitered edge, for instance. From the wrong side, insert the needle into the fold of the fabric and pull the thread. Work from right to left as you pick up just a thread or two in one fold and then insert the needle into the fold opposite the first stitch. Repeat, making stitches every ¼ inch or so.

There are several other hand stitches you may find useful. The tack is simply a straight stitch used to join layers of fabric. You can repeat them in place, or make a series of straight stitches. Use a series of tacks to sew on a curtain ring, for example. The backstitch is a stitch worked from left to right, with each stitch ending at the edge of the previous stitch. It's a sturdy stitch because the thread overlaps on the back side of the fabric.

Finish a line of hand stitching in one of two ways. Make a series of small backstitches repeated several times in place. You can also make a quick knot. Make a wee stitch on top of your last stitch on the wrong side of your fabric, forming a small loop. Pull the needle through the loop until a second loop forms. Pull the needle through the second loop tightly to form a knot.

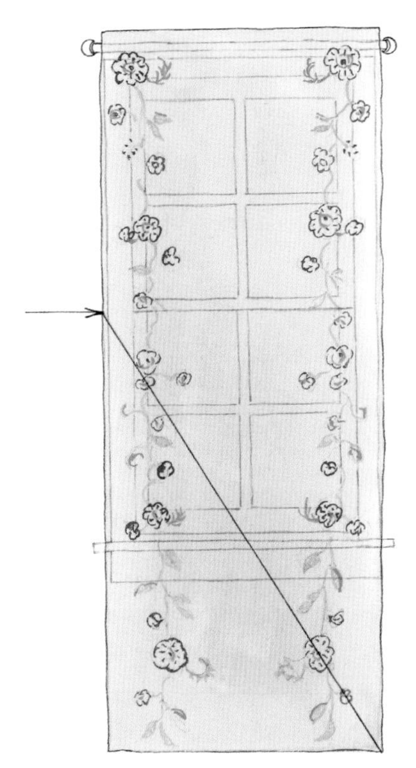

Planning the hem for the Sarong Curtain (page 54)

Check the fit

Does this seem like a silly idea? On the contrary, fitting your window treatments before you hem the bottom is probably a good idea, at least until you feel confident with your measuring and sewing skills. If you need to tweak the hem allowance, it's easier to do it *before* you've stitched the hem than after! However, if you've measured carefully, cut out carefully, and stitched carefully, your window treatment should fit.

Fix a mistake

The trick to making curtains successfully is all in the measurement, as most of the sewing is fairly straightforward. However, we all make mistakes, even the most experienced seamstresses (especially when our caffeine level is low). There's not much that can't be repaired by simply ripping out all the stitches and trying again. When you're using a seam ripper to remove stitches, be careful not to tear the fabric by ripping too enthusiastically. I know how much fun it can be (she says sarcastically).

If you're having a weak moment and feel unsure about something you've just stitched, chill a second and make sure it's correct before you do any trimming or clipping.

Embellish Your Curtain

Photo 1

Sometimes a window treatment needs a little TLC to make it extra special. The expanse of a curtain panel is the perfect canvas to decorate, and the embellishments you add offer you another opportunity to express your style. Here are a few ways that we've adorned our window treatments.

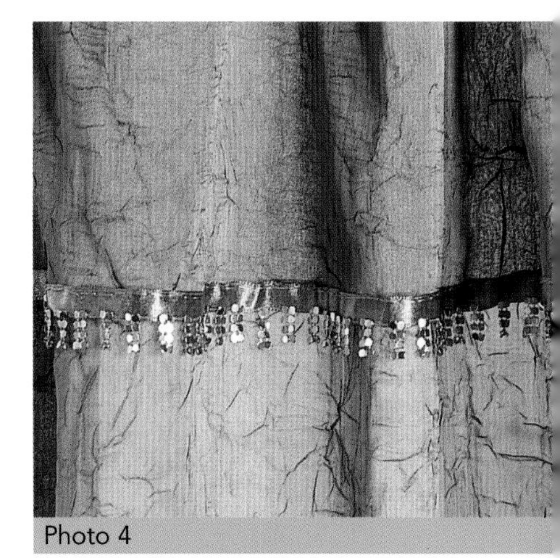

Photo 4

An obvious choice is to add decorative trim to make your curtain more beautiful. We merely stitched this luxurious trim onto the front of the curtain as a finishing touch (photo 1). You can use decorative stitching when you're sewing, too (photo 2). Experiment with the placement and pin the trim or fabric in place before you begin, if necessary. And have some fun with trim, too, as we did in the valance project (photo 3). We stitched on the sparkly trim in photo 4 by hand, using a line of backstitches.

Photo 2

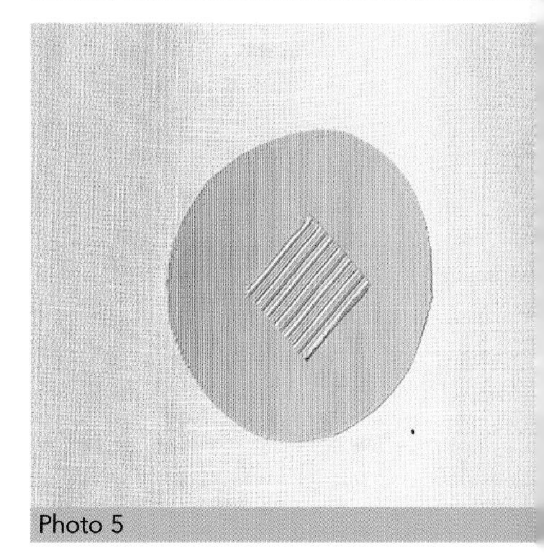

Photo 5

Photo 3

We had a lot of fun with appliqués in this book—we stitched 'em on, we fused 'em on, and we decorated 'em with embroidery. If you fuse them on, which is a very quick and easy way to add appliqués to your curtains, be sure your fabric can withstand the heat of the fusing process. And of course, you can fuse them and *then* stitch them too, as the fusing holds them in place and makes the stitching a bit easier. Your appliqués can be graphic (photo 5) or somewhat realistic (photo 6) or something in between.

Finally, you just can't write a book about curtains without including a ruffle or two. We have some ruffles in our café curtain (photo 7) that offer a modern deconstructed twist; these ruffles have raw edges. This border of silk ribbon has casual ruffles every so often that lend a romantic feel to these linen curtains (photo 8).

Because we've grown quite fond of you, we've included some additional techniques you can use to embellish your curtains on page 106. It's free with the purchase of *Fun & Fabulous Curtains!*

Photo 6

Photo 7

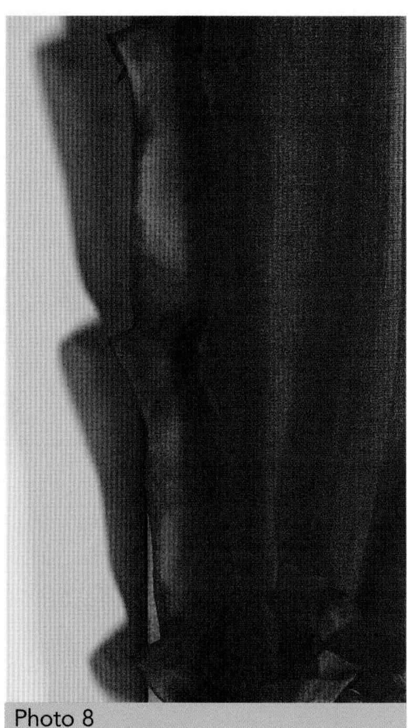
Photo 8

Use This Book

Alright, people, we've discussed just about everything you really need to know about making a curtain. We've looked at how-to photographs and illustrations, we've had some java, and I'm just about ready to turn it over to you. Here are a few things to keep in mind before you start to sew.

CHOOSE YOUR PROJECT. We've offered several different ways to make your window treatments, from simple rod-pocket construction to more involved pleated headings. But remember all the other variations we talked about—using tabs or ties, adding grommets, decorating your window treatment—and think about what you want your curtains to look like. We invite you to peruse all 15 of our projects before you decide how to start.

Generally speaking, the projects are presented in categories according to ease of construction. The icons will rate the ease of the project, and the key on page 51 explains which skills are included in each category. As the projects progress, techniques are added so you'll have gained a repertoire of sewing skills by the end of the book. See pages 52 and 53 for a quick preview of each curtain.

FOLLOW THE INSTRUCTIONS. Purchase the fabric and notions according to our project instructions. This is important: remember that you'll have to measure your windows and determine the basic width and length of your window treatments. We've provided you with the allowances we added for hems and so forth, but these figures will have to be added to the measurements that you determine from your own windows.

We have a few projects that have panels made from different fabrics, so when the instructions say, "Determine the proportion of the panels to one another," we mean measure and decide on the size of each panel as it best fits your window. (The simplest way to do this will be to figure the total yardage you need, and then divide that into the individual increments. We'll provide the measurements from our projects for moral support.) Of course, we'll give you the directions that we used to make our curtains, including some witty commentary along the way. Our how-to illustrations will make it a breeze to follow the instructions.

Naturally, it's very unlikely that you'll be making curtains for windows that are the same size as the ones we used. However, we've also given you some hints so you can judge how the designs might look on your windows. We used four different windows for our projects, and here are the dimensions, including the trim:

Window #1—40 x 61 inches

Window #2—36 x 62 inches

Window #3—55 x 55½ inches

Window #4—51¼ x 55¼ inches

In addition to telling you which window we used, our instructions will also give the fullness of the design (the 1X, 1.5X, and 2X stuff from page 11); and the number of panels we used.

PREPARE TO SEW. Now that you've got everything you need to begin making your curtain, arrange your tools and materials within easy reach. There's nothing worse than squinting while you're sewing, so treat yourself to adequate lighting in your workspace.

Speaking of tools and materials, you'll see a list for each of our projects. However, we're not going to list every single little supply you need for each curtain, but rather refer you to this list of basic tools and materials. So, have the following on hand for any simply irresistible project in our Make a Curtain! section:

- sewing machine
- machine needles
- measuring tools
- marking tools
- scissors
- seam ripper
- pins
- needles for hand sewing
- thread
- iron & ironing board

Before you start to sew, repeat your mantra—measure twice, and cut once. And remember to use ½-inch seams, unless otherwise noted.

Only a few more pages of handy information and we'll be ready to make lots of fabulous curtains.

Anatomy of a Curtain

It's *so* easy to make a curtain. Who knew?

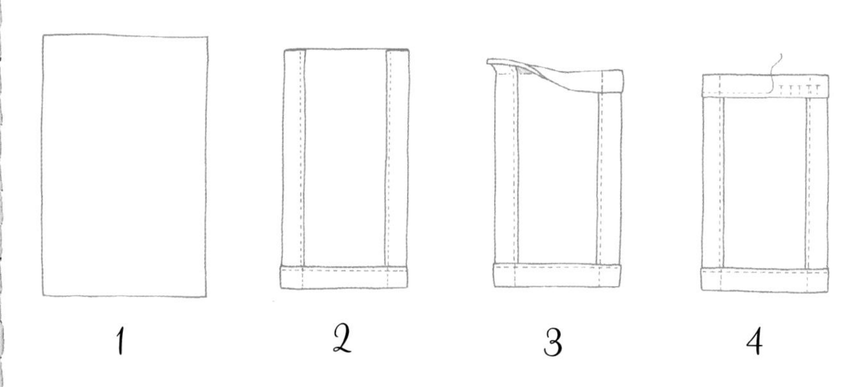

1 Measure your window and add allowances for side and bottom hems. Cut out your panels to match your measurements.

2 Make double hems on the sides and the bottom.

3 To make a rod pocket casing, press under several inches at the top and turn under ½ inch on the raw edge.

4 Pin and stitch the casing in place.

Wow! Your first curtain panel is complete. Sit back and admire.

Icon Key

Each of our projects is rated according to ease of construction. (Please note that I didn't say *difficulty* of construction.) Here's how we've organized them.

ABSOLUTE BEGINNER

Suitable for the first-time sewer.

BASIC SKILLS YOU'LL USE:

Right sides together (page 38)

Double hem (page 39)

Add a header (page 39)

Making tabs (page 40)

EASY BEGINNER

Suitable for the new sewer who understands the basics and is ready for more fun.

NEW SKILLS YOU'LL USE:

Trim seams and clip curves (page 35)

Make a French seam (page 37)

Make a very narrow hem (page 38)

Add grommets (page 42)

Add a ruffle (page 44)

EXPERIENCED BEGINNER

Suitable for the sewer who's mastered the basics and is ready to redecorate the neighborhood.

NEW SKILLS YOU'LL USE:

Use heading tape (page 42)

Add pleats (page 44)

Add a facing (page 44)

Tip

A tip offers you a nifty idea.

Why?

Wondering why you're doing something? Here's the answer.

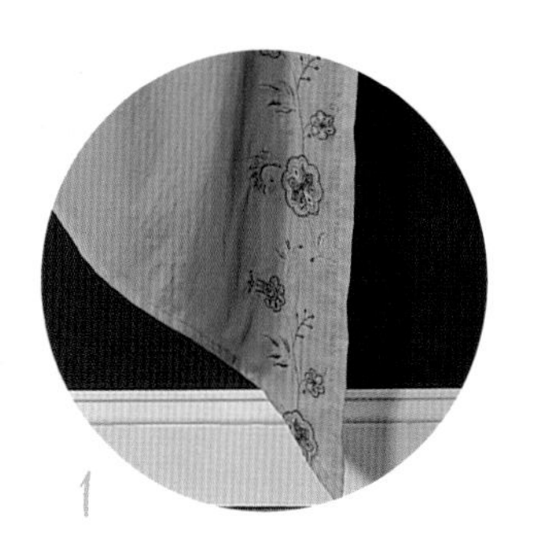
1

2

3

4

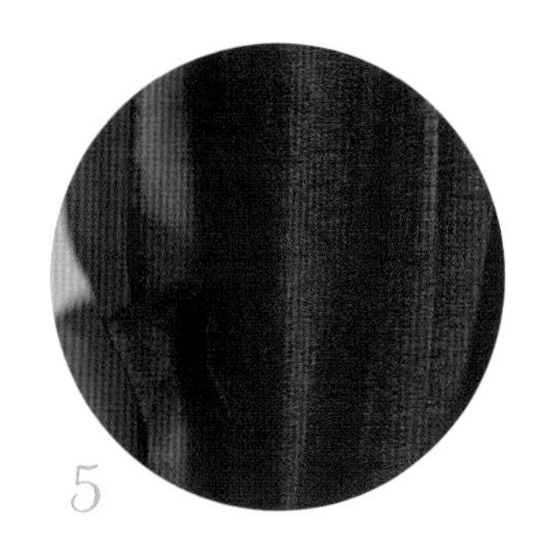
5

6

7

Curtain Preview

Here's a peek at our collection of window treatment projects.

1. **SARONG CURTAIN.** It doesn't get any easier than this design that features an asymmetrical hem and a fabulous embroidered fabric.

2. **SIMPLE PRINT CURTAINS.** This great beginner's project features a beautiful print.

3. **LAYERS OF LINEN.** Use layers of fabric in different colors to create a breezy window treatment.

4. **EASY SHADE.** It's not quite a shade, and not quite a curtain—you decide.

5. **VALENTINE CURTAIN.** What a difference a little hand-dyed silk ribbon can make. See for yourself.

6. **CAFÉ CURTAIN.** Edgy in a good way, this little curtain features deconstructed details and ruffles too.

7. **GROOVY GROMMETS.** This project is loud, proud, and thoroughly hip in every way.

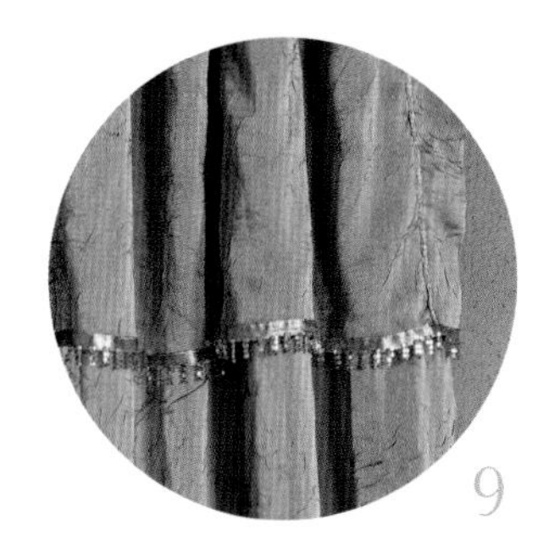

9

11

13

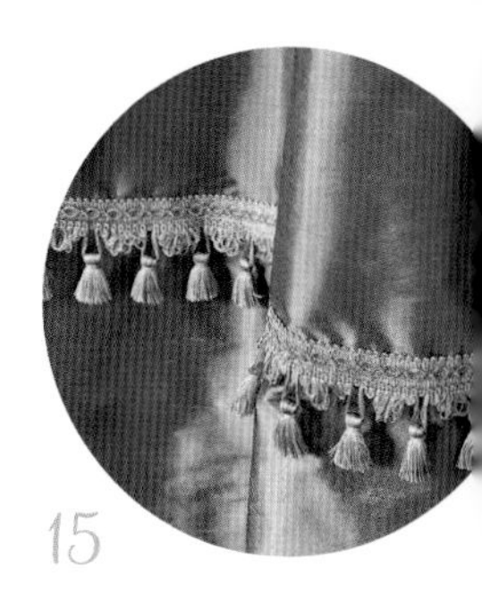

15

8

10

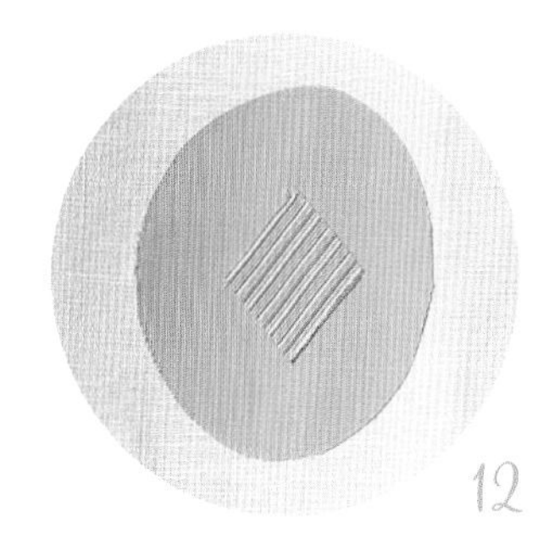

12

14

8. **BLOOMING CURTAINS.** A little whimsy, anyone? This project (for a wee one's room, perhaps) has all the fanciful details you can imagine.

9. **BELLY DANCER DRAPES.** These easy drapes have embellishment details to die for. Or at least to dance for.

10. **STYLISH SWAG.** Two great fabrics + a reversible design = irresistible charm.

11. **EDGY CURTAINS.** For this project, use an unusual approach to cutting—don't! Tear the fabric instead.

12. **GREEN MEDALLION CURTAINS.** Add appliqués and mix-and-match fabrics to create the perfect contemporary window treatment.

13. **ROMANTIC ROMAN SHADE.** Here's a brilliantly easy take on a classic design.

14. **PLEATED CURTAINS.** This sophisticated project pairs an elegant fabric with a traditional dressmaking technique.

15. **ELEGANT SILK DRAPERIES.** Luxurious silk panels make a memorable window treatment. Just you wait and see.

It's as easy as it looks.

Sarong Curtain

Have a little fun with your first curtain, a playful creation that lets a little window peek through.

WHAT YOU NEED

- Basic curtain-making tools and supplies
- Fabric to fit your window (we used 3 yards of embroidered cotton voile)
- Matching thread

CURTAIN SPECS

- Window #1
- Width 1.5X
- 1 panel

ABSOLUTE BEGINNER

Cheat sheet for absolute beginner on page 51

HOW YOU MAKE IT

1 Measure your window, include the appropriate allowances for hems and heading, and calculate your yardage according to the instructions on pages 18 and 19. We added the following allowances to the panel: to the width, 2 inches for the side hems; and to the length, ½ inch for the lower hem and 3 inches for the rod-pocket casing.

If your fabric has embroidered edges as ours did, be sure to cut away the selvages so the fabric lies as flat as possible (figure 1). Then cut out one full-length panel based on your measurements; you'll trim away the excess in step 5.

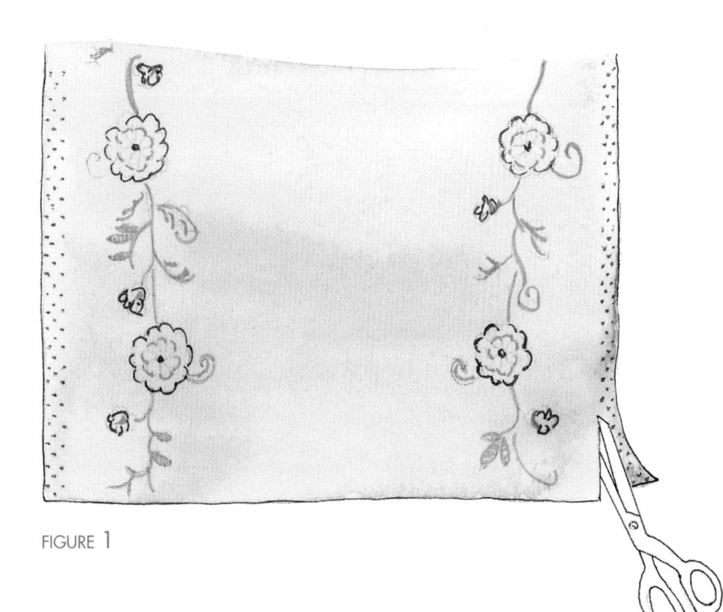

FIGURE 1

FIGURE 2

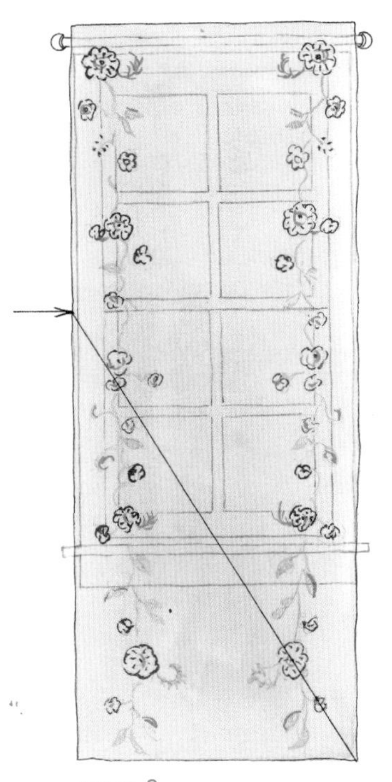

FIGURE 3

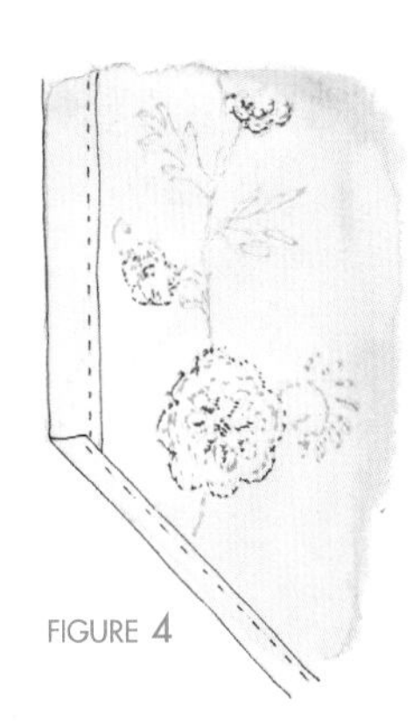

FIGURE 4

2 Make ½-inch double hems at each side, folding under 1 inch and pressing, then folding the raw edge in to meet the fold. Press, pin, and stitch (figure 2).

3 Create the casing at the top. Press under 3 inches, and then turn under ½ inch on the raw edge. Press. Pin in place and stitch.

4 Put the curtain on your window to decide where to trim away the excess fabric and form the asymmetrical hem. Mark (figure 3) and remove.

5 Trim away the fabric and make a ¼-inch double hem at the bottom edge, using the same method you used in step 2. Fold under the edges as shown (figure 4).

Simple Print Curtains

Can the easiest thing you could possibly make also be the most beautiful? You be the judge.

WHAT YOU NEED

Basic curtain-making tools and supplies

Fabric to fit your window (we used 6 yards of lightweight cotton)

Matching thread

CURTAIN SPECS

Window #4

Width 1.5X

2 panels

ABSOLUTE BEGINNER

Cheat sheet for absolute beginner on page 51

HOW YOU MAKE IT

1 Measure your window, include the appropriate allowances for hems and heading, and calculate your yardage according to the instructions on pages 18 and 19. We added the following allowances to each panel: to the width, 8 inches for the side hems; and to the length, 6 inches for the lower hem, and 3 inches for the rod-pocket casing. Since the length of this curtain is critical, hitting just at the bottom of the sill, we factored in an additional 5/8 inch for the take-up allowance.

Cut out two panels based on your measurements.

2 Make a 2-inch double hem at each side, folding under 4 inches and pressing, then folding the raw edge in to meet the fold. Press, pin, and stitch (figure 1).

3 Create the casing at the top of each panel. Press under 3 inches, and then turn under 1/2 inch on the raw edge. Press (figure 2). Pin in place and stitch (figure 3).

4 Make a 3-inch double hem at the bottom of each panel, using the same method you used in step 2.

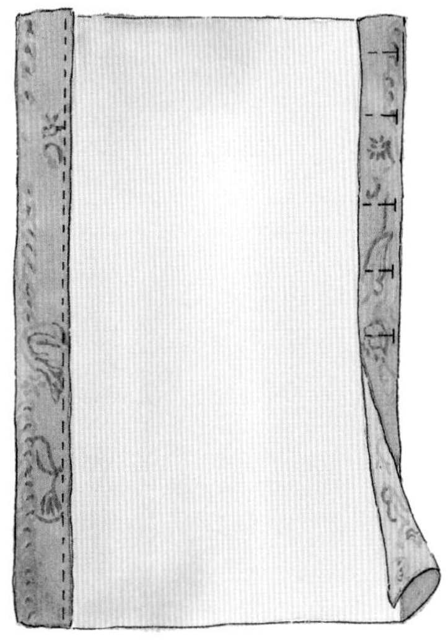
FIGURE 1

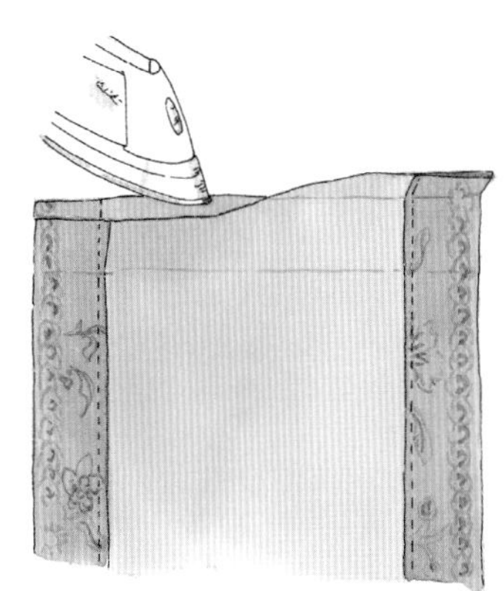
FIGURE 2

FIGURE 3

Why?

Why hold the fabric up to the light before you buy it? Here's why—see how the pattern in this fabric pops when light shines through.

Understated chic, breezy beauty.

Layers of *Linen*

Simple yet elegant, these layered curtains are sewn in lovely linen embroidered with delicate flowers.

HOW YOU MAKE IT

1 Measure your window, include the appropriate allowances for hems and headings, and calculate your yardage according to the instructions on pages 18 and 19. We added the following allowances to each panel: to the width, 2 inches for the side hems; and to the length, 1 inch for the upper hem and 1 inch for the lower hem.

Cut two wide panels based on your measurements; cut two narrow panels half the width of the wide panels, but the same length.

We also cut 14 tabs that were each 5 x 14 inches, using the same fabric as the wide panel.

2 Make 1/2-inch double hems at each side of each panel, folding under 1 inch and pressing, then folding the raw edge in to meet the fold. Press, pin, and stitch (figure 1).

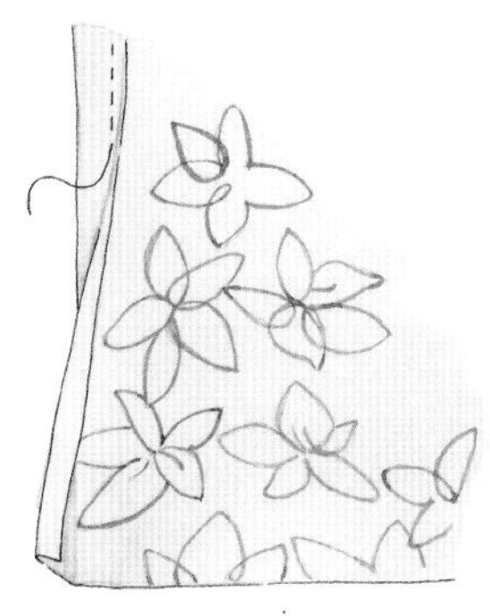

FIGURE 1

3 Place a narrow panel on top of a wide one, both with right sides up and their top and left sides aligned. Baste along the top edge. Repeat with the remaining panels, but align their *right sides.*

WHAT YOU NEED

- Basic curtain-making tools and supplies
- Fabric to fit your window (we used 6 1/2 yards of linen for the wide panel and 3 yards of linen for the narrow panel)
- Matching thread

CURTAIN SPECS

- Window #3
- Width 2x
- 2 panels

ABSOLUTE BEGINNER

Cheat sheet for absolute beginner on page 51

FIGURE 2

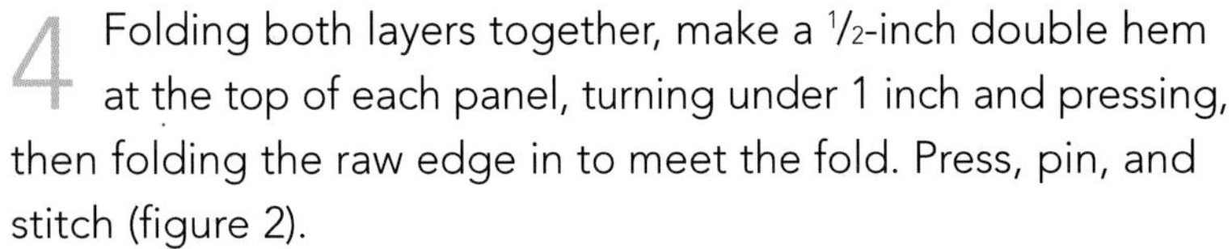

4 Folding both layers together, make a ½-inch double hem at the top of each panel, turning under 1 inch and pressing, then folding the raw edge in to meet the fold. Press, pin, and stitch (figure 2).

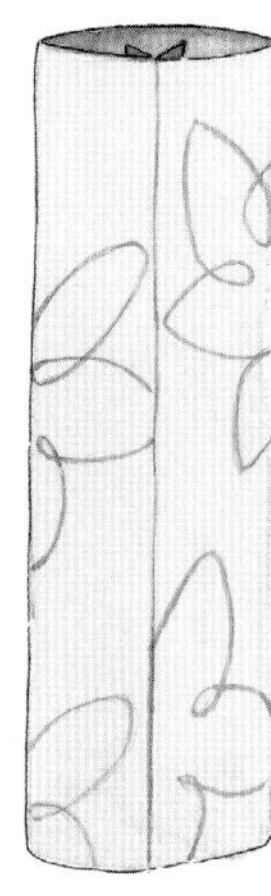

FIGURE 3

5 To make the tabs, take one piece and fold it in half lengthwise, right sides together. Stitch in a ½-inch seam. Turn the tab right side out, placing the seam in the center of the back of the tab (figure 3).

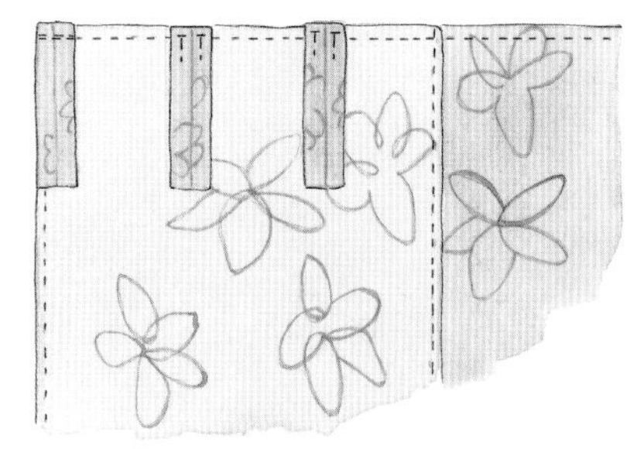

FIGURE 4

6 Determine the placement of the tabs and mark as desired. Place one at the edge of each side hem, and space the others approximately 6 to 8 inches apart, placing the raw edges of the tabs along the top of the curtain. Pin and stitch each tab in place following the hemstitching line (figure 4). Fold under ½ inch on the raw edges of each tab and fold to the back of the curtain. Pin and stitch in place along the hemstitching line.

7 Make a ½-inch double hem at the bottom of each panel, folding under 1 inch and pressing, then folding the raw edge in to meet the fold. Press, pin, and stitch.

Easy Shade

When you want to dress a window and enjoy your view, too, consider this gauzy window treatment.

It's as short or as long as your heart desires.

WHAT YOU NEED

Basic curtain-making tools and supplies

Fabric to fit your window (we used 3/4 yard of linen/cotton blend, 1 1/2 yards of sheer fabric, and 1/4 yard of striped linen/cotton blend for the ties)

Matching thread

CURTAIN SPECS

Window #1

Width 1X

1 panel

EASY BEGINNER

Cheat sheet for easy beginner on page 51

Tip

FYI, our shade is almost floor length, so we have plenty of the sheer fabric to gather up in the ties.

HOW YOU MAKE IT

1 Measure your windows, include the appropriate allowances for hems and headings, and calculate your yardage according to the instructions on pages 18 and 19. We added the following allowances to the shade: to the width, 2 inches for the side hems; determine the proportion of the panels to one another (the linen panel should be from one-third to one-fourth the length of your window) and to these dimensions, add 3⅝ inches to the linen panel for the header and the seam allowance, and 3⅝ inches to the sheer panel for the bottom hem and the seam allowance.

Cut out the linen panel and the sheer panel based on your measurements. We also cut four ties that were each 1½ x 55 inches; you'll add two ties to the front of the shade and two ties to the back of the shade.

2 To make the ties for the back, fold under ¼ inch on each short end and press. Fold under ¼ inch on each long edge and press (figure 1), and then fold the fabric in half lengthwise. Press and pin. Topstitch along the edges. Make the ties for the front as those for the back, but turn under ¼ inch on one short end *only*, leaving the other end with raw edges.

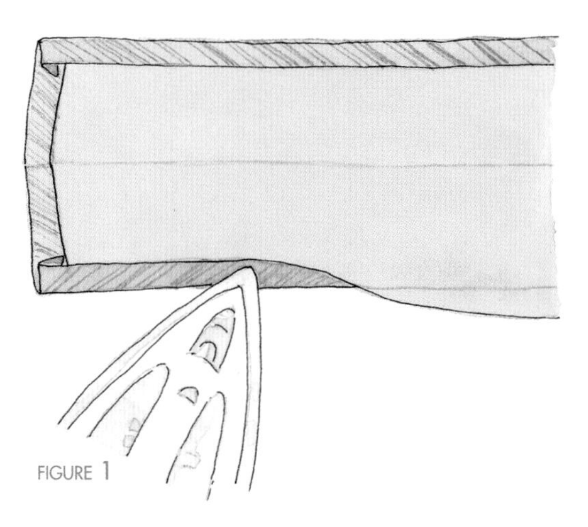

FIGURE 1

3 Stitch the linen panel to the sheer panel with a 5/8-inch French seam. Begin by stitching the *wrong* sides together in a 1/4-inch seam. Trim the seam and turn the fabric inside out so the right sides are together. Before you finish the French seam, you'll attach the ties.

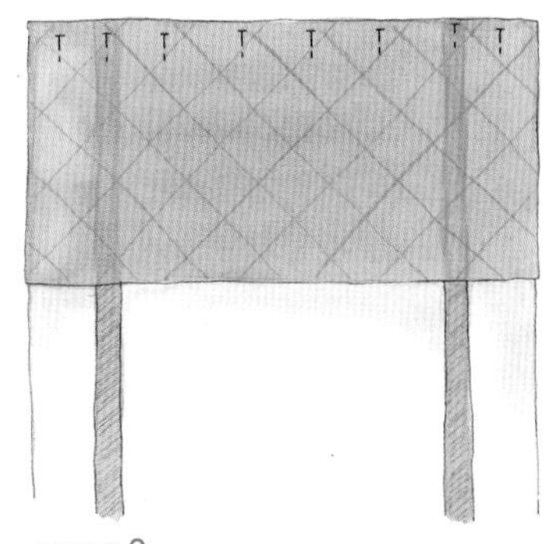
FIGURE 2

4 Mark the location of the ties; our ties are about 8 inches from the side edges. Place the front ties between the panels, with the ends with the raw edges butting up to the seam (figure 2). Stitch together in a 3/8-inch seam, encasing the raw edges of the seams and the ends of ties. Press the seam toward the linen panel.

5 Make 1/2-inch double hems at each side of the shade, folding under 1 inch and pressing, then folding the raw edge in to meet the fold. Press, pin, and stitch.

FIGURE 3

6 Hem the bottom of the curtain by pressing under 3 inches, and then turning under 1/2 inch on the raw edge. Press. Pin in place and stitch.

7 Add the remaining ties to the back of the shade, matching their placement to those on the front. Pin the ties in place (figure 3) and baste. Topstitch the French seam to the linen panel, sewing the ties in place at the same time. Remove the basting stitches.

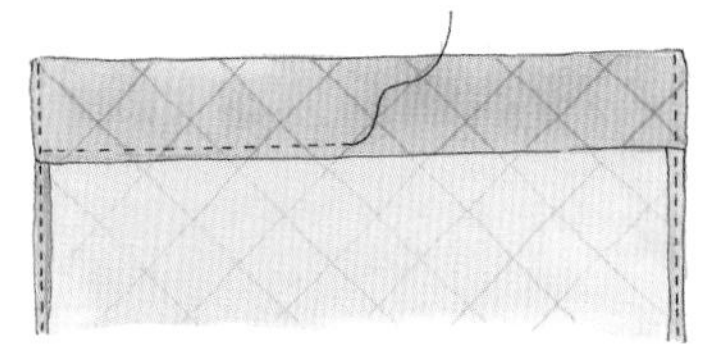
FIGURE 4

8 Create the casing at the top. Press under 3 inches, and then turn under 1/2 inch on the raw edge. Press. Pin in place and stitch (figure 4).

9 After hanging the shade, gather and tie as desired.

Fall in love all over again.

Valentine Curtain

If your life is lacking romance, add a little with this lovely window treatment. Trim the edges in silk ribbon for the coup de grâce.

WHAT YOU NEED

Basic curtain-making tools and supplies

Fabric and trim to fit your window (we used 2½ yards of lightweight linen and 6 yards of 1½-inch hand-dyed silk ribbon)

Matching thread

CURTAIN SPECS

Window #2

Width 1.5X

1 panel

EASY BEGINNER

Cheat sheet for easy beginner on page 51

HOW YOU MAKE IT

1 Measure your window, include the appropriate allowances for hems and heading, and calculate your yardage according to the instructions on pages 18 and 19. We added the following allowances to the panel: to the width, 4 inches for the side hems; and to the length, 4 inches for the lower hem and 3½ inches for the rod-pocket casing and header.

Cut out one panel based on your measurements.

2 Make 1-inch double hems at each side, folding under 2 inches and pressing, then folding the raw edge in to meet the fold. Press, pin, and stitch.

3 Add the variegated ribbon accents to the edges of the curtain, beginning at the left side. We made casual pleats in the silk ribbon every 4 inches or so (and we do mean *or so*) and stitched the ribbon onto the outside of the curtain, aligning the edge of the ribbon with the stitching line of the hemmed edges. To make the pleats without elaborate measuring and marking, align the curtain with a long measuring tool (a yardstick or a cutting mat) and pin the pleats at the appropriate intervals (figure 1). Slide the curtain to pleat along the length. Our pleats are approximately (and we do mean *approximately*) 1 inch wide.

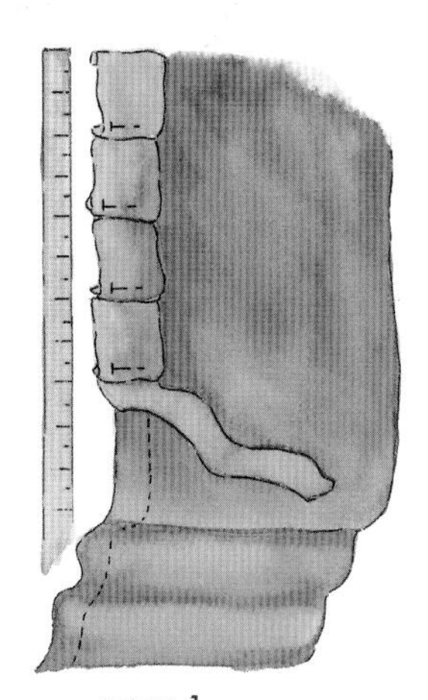

FIGURE 1

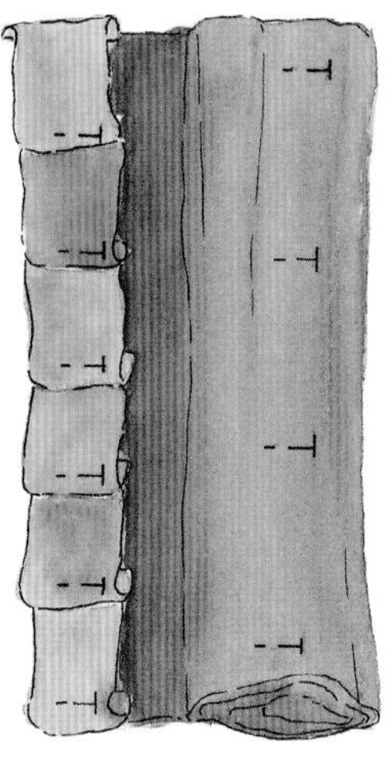

FIGURE 2

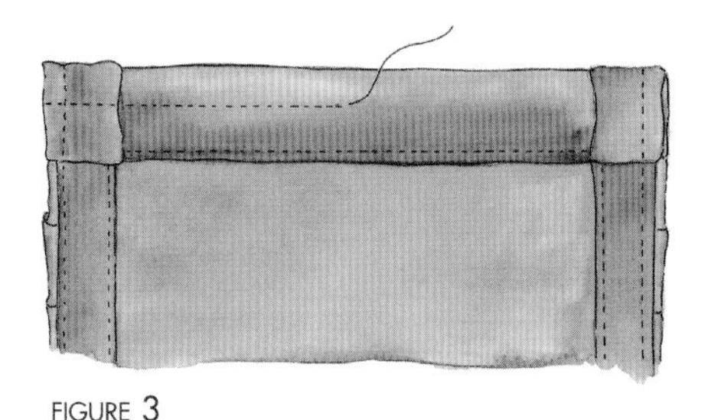

FIGURE 3

4 To manipulate the width of the fabric while you stitch the ribbon onto the left side of the curtain, make a loose fold of about 6 inches and then roll the fabric up close to the left edge, securing with a few pins (figure 2). Stitch the ribbon to the left edge about 1/2 inch from the inner edge of the ribbon. Be sure to stitch the ribbon on in the same direction on each side (down the length).

5 Unpin the curtain width and add the ribbon to the right side, pinning and stitching as in steps 3 and 4 above.

6 Create the casing at the top. Press under 3 1/2 inches, and then turn under 1/2 inch on the raw edge. Press. Pin in place and stitch. To create the header, turn the curtain to the wrong side. Mark 1 1/2 inches from the top and stitch along this line (figure 3).

7 Make 2-inch double hems at the bottom, using the same method you used in step 2.

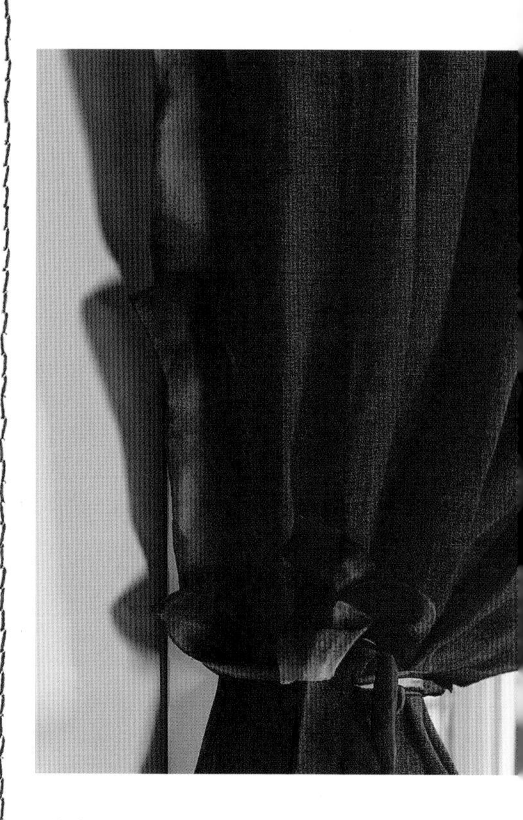

Tip

We designed this window treatment as a single panel, which could either gather at the side or hang languorously in the center of the window, exposing part of the window frame and allowing some light to seep in. If you'd prefer to hide your window, add a second panel for complete coverage.

Café Curtain

The raw edges on these ruffles lend contemporary flair to a traditional window treatment. The charm lies in mixing and matching fabrics.

WHAT YOU NEED

- Basic curtain-making tools and supplies
- Fabric to fit your window (we used 3/4 yard of lightweight cotton for the curtain, 1/2 yard for the large bottom ruffle, and 1/4 yard for the small ruffles)
- Matching thread
- Café clip rings
- Tension rod

CURTAIN SPECS

- Window #2
- Width 1X
- 1 panel

EASY BEGINNER

Cheat sheet for easy beginner on page 51

A snap to stitch

Tip

In the interest of full disclosure, we admit that this curtain is a just a teeny bit wider than 1X since we used the entire width of the fabric without any additional cutting. Thus, this design can accommodate windows that are less wide—but not wider—than the fabric itself. For example, our fabric was 44 inches wide, and our window was 36 inches wide, so we have some gentle gathers in our café curtain.

HOW YOU MAKE IT

1 Since you can adjust a tension rod to hang anywhere in a window, you don't have to do any complicated calculations for this curtain. Measure from the top to the bottom of your window, and divide this figure in half. This will be the length of your curtain (minus the bottom ruffle); round that number to the nearest $^1/_8$ yard and purchase that amount of fabric (27 inches = $^3/_4$ yard, for example) and use it as is—no additional cutting is necessary.

For the large bottom ruffles, cut enough 6-inch-wide strips to equal 3 and one-half times the width of your finished curtain. For the smaller ruffles, cut enough 2-inch-wide strips to make two strips that are each 2 and one-half times the width of your finished curtain.

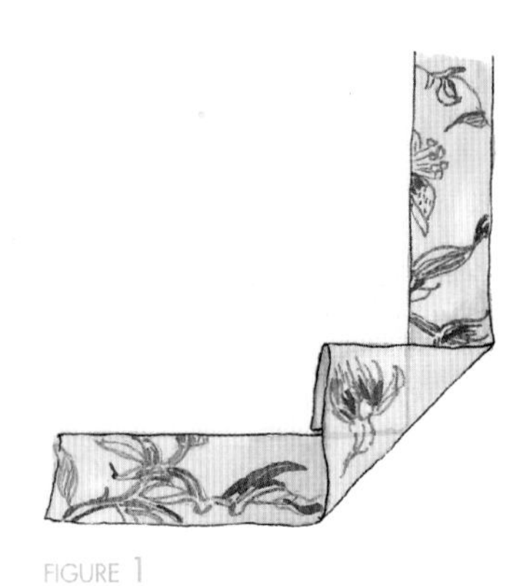

FIGURE 1

2 Make 1-inch double hems at the top and the sides of the curtain, mitering the edges. Fold under 2 inches and press, then fold the raw edge in to meet the fold. Press the double hem in place. To miter, undo the second fold and fold the corner diagonally at the spot where the two fold lines intersect; the previous fold lines and the seam should align (figure 1). Press the corner. Trim away the excess fabric, leaving about $^1/_2$ inch. Fold back into the mitered edge. Press, pin, and stitch the hems.

Groovy Grommets

Oversized grommets and a bold print lend a casual, modern look to any interior.

WHAT YOU NEED

- Basic curtain-making tools and supplies
- Fabric to fit your window (we used 6 yards of heavy-weight cotton)
- Matching thread
- Grommet tape and decorative rings

CURTAIN SPECS

- Window #1
- Width 1.5X
- 2 panels

EASY BEGINNER

Cheat sheet for easy beginner on page 51

HOW YOU MAKE IT

1 Measure your window, include the appropriate allowances for hems and headings, and calculate your yardage according to the instructions on pages 18 and 19. We added the following allowances to each panel: to the width, 8 inches for the side hems; and to the length, 5 inches for the top hem and 8 inches for the bottom hem.

Cut out two panels based on your measurements.

2 Center the grommet tape on your panels between the side hemlines, making sure to have an even number of grommets on each curtain (figure 1). You may need to alter the width of your side hems depending on how much space you have between the grommets and the fabric edge.

3 Create the casing at the top of each panel. Press under 5 inches, and then turn under 1/2 inch on the raw edge. Press. Pin in place and stitch.

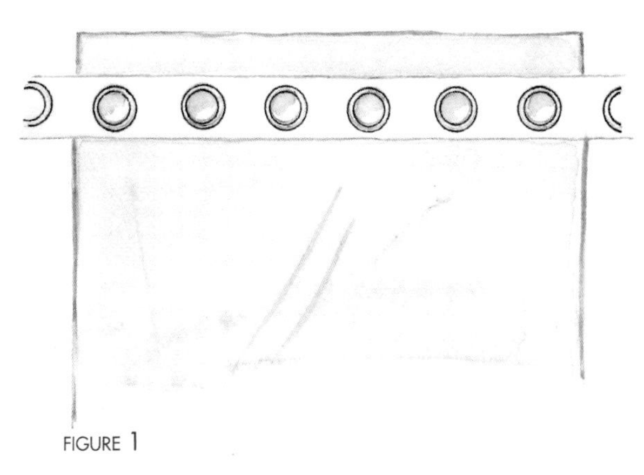

FIGURE 1

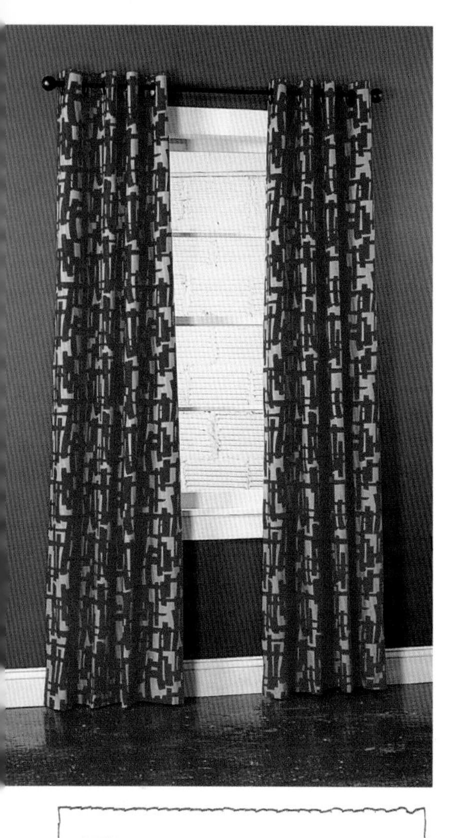

4 Follow the manufacturer's instructions for applying the grommet tape. With the type we used, we stitched the tape to the curtain along each edge (figure 2). We then trimmed away the fabric inside the grommets (figure 3) and snapped on decorative rings.

5 Make 1-inch double hems on the sides by folding under 2 inches and pressing, then folding the raw edge in to meet the fold. Press, pin, and stitch.

6 Make a 4-inch double hem on each panel by folding under 8 inches and pressing, then folding the raw edge in to meet the fold. Press, pin, and stitch. You can hang the curtains flat, or gather them into nice crisp folds (figure 4).

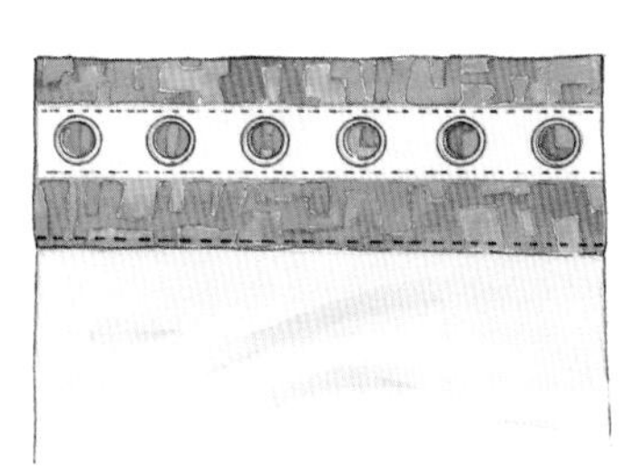

FIGURE 2

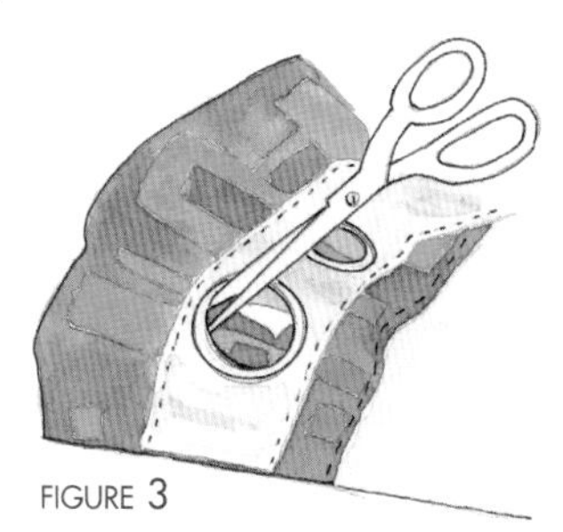

FIGURE 3

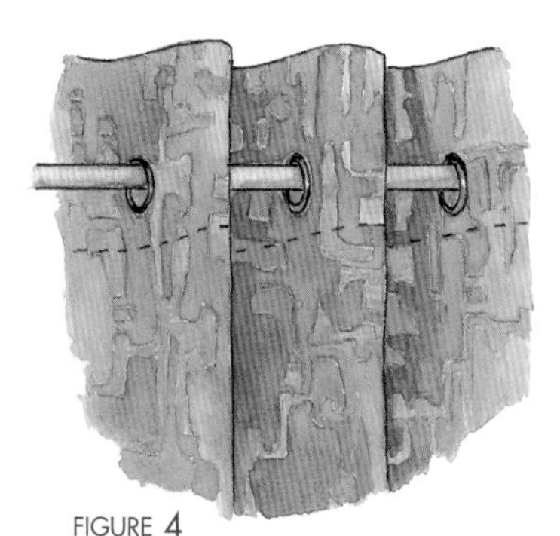

FIGURE 4

Tip

While we've given you general directions on applying grommet tape, be sure to read the instructions that come with the product you buy before you purchase the fabric for your curtain panels. Because these products vary by manufacturer, our directions may not be appropriate for the tape you're using. Word to the wise!

Blooming Curtains

With these decorated curtains in your windows, you'll have spring fever year 'round.

WHAT YOU NEED

- Basic curtain-making tools and supplies
- Fabric and trim to fit your window (we used 2½ yards each of two differently colored sheer fabrics A and B, assorted ribbons and rickrack, embroidery floss, a variety of brightly patterned fabric scraps, and a selection of buttons and beads)
- Invisible thread and matching thread
- Approximately 2 yards of paper-backed fusible web
- Water-soluble fabric glue
- Embroidery needle

CURTAIN SPECS

- Window #4
- Width 1X
- 2 panels

EASY BEGINNER

Cheat sheet for easy beginner on page 51

FIGURE 1

HOW YOU MAKE IT

1 Measure your windows, include the appropriate allowances for hems and headings, and calculate your yardage according to the instructions on pages 18 and 19. The fabrics will overlap in the center third of each panel (figure 1), so each fabric piece is two-thirds of the length of the window plus allowances. We added the following allowances to each panel: to the width, 4 inches for the side hems; and to the bottom fabric A, 8 inches for the lower hem, and to the top fabric B, 6 inches for the rod-pocket casing and header.

Cut out two A pieces and two B pieces based on your measurements.

2 Cut two pieces of the fusible web that are as wide as your panels and one-third the length of the A pieces. Iron them to the wrong side of the top of the fabric A pieces, following the manufacturer's instructions. Don't remove the paper backing yet!

3 On the paper backing, draw flower and leaf motifs (figure 2). Cut the background away. Remove the paper backings from the motifs, saving them to use later.

4 Measure and mark a line that's 2½ inches from the bottom of each fabric B piece. With the adhesive facing the right side of the fabric B piece, put the fabric A pieces (with the flower motifs) on the fabric B pieces, placing the bottoms of the fusible web along the marked lines. Fuse the pieces together, following the manufacturer's instructions.

5 Press the 2½-inch unfused section of the fabric B pieces toward the top of the curtain. Turn under ½ inch on the raw edges. Press, pin, and stitch. (You'll be working on the back of the curtain.)

6 Topstitch along the flower edges, using invisible thread as the top thread and thread to match the fabric in the bobbin (figure 3).

7 Make 1-inch double hems at each side by folding under 2 inches and pressing, then folding the raw edge in to meet the fold. Press, pin, and stitch, using the appropriate color of thread in the bobbin.

8 Create the casing at the top of each panel. Press under 6 inches, and then turn under ½ inch on the raw edge. Press, pin, and stitch. To create the header, turn the curtain to the wrong side. Mark a line that's 1½ inches from the top and stitch along this line.

FIGURE 2

FIGURE 3

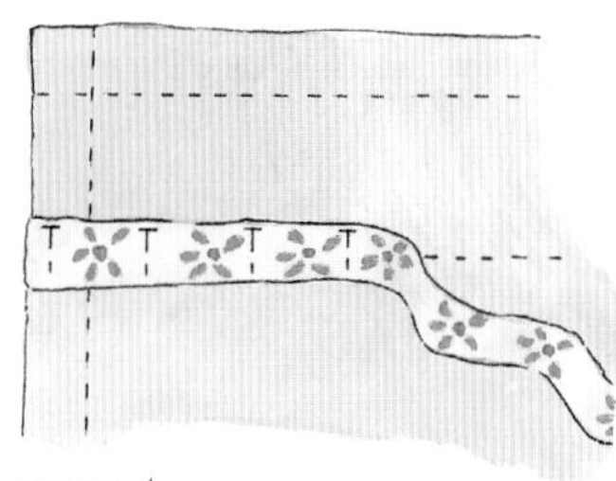

FIGURE 4

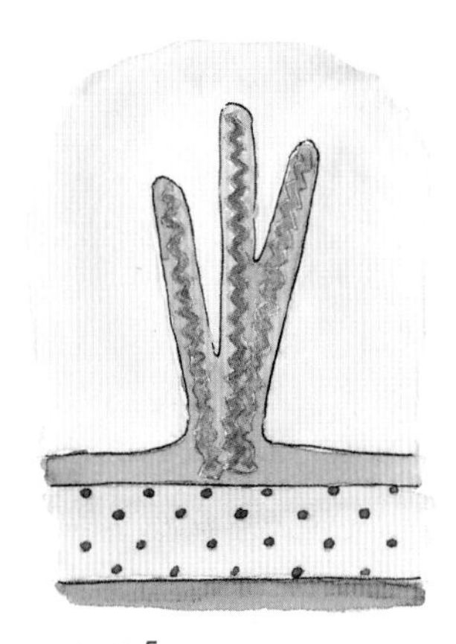

FIGURE 5

FIGURE 6

9 Pin ribbon across the top of each panel, covering the hem stitching (figure 4), and stitch along each edge of the ribbon. Fold the ends of the ribbon to the back as you stitch.

10 Using the paper backings from step 3 as patterns, cut flower shapes out of the assorted scraps. Casually position them on top of the flowers on the curtains, leaving some curtain fabric exposed as desired. Hold the flower shapes in place temporarily with water-soluble glue. Make stems and leaves from the ribbon and rickrack, also holding them in place with glue (figure 5). Topstitch along the edges of each element. Hand stitch buttons or beads in the centers of the flowers, and embroider on the petals as desired (figure 6).

11 Make 4-inch double hems at the bottoms using the same technique you used in step 7.

Belly Dancer Drapes

These alluring curtains add some mystery to your room. (And a little shimmy, too!)

Twinkle, twinkle, little trim.

WHAT YOU NEED

- Basic curtain-making tools and supplies
- Fabric and trim to fit your window (we used 6½ yards of crinkle synthetic, 4 yards of ¼-inch braid, and 3 yards of beaded trim)
- Matching thread
- Drapery clip rings

CURTAIN SPECS

- Window #1
- Width 1.5X
- 2 panels

EASY BEGINNER

Cheat sheet for easy beginner on page 51

HOW YOU MAKE IT

1 Measure your windows, include the appropriate allowances for hems and heading, and calculate your yardage according to the instructions on pages 18 and 19. We added the following allowances to each panel: to the width, 8 inches for the side hems; and to the length, 6 inches for the lower hem, 8 inches for puddling, and 14 inches for the self-valance (it should be about 1/6 of the measurement to the floor). See figure 1 for a diagram of this panel.

Cut out two panels based on your measurements.

2 Make 2-inch double hems at each side, folding under 4 inches and pressing, then folding the raw edge in to meet the fold. Press, pin, and stitch.

3 The valances of these drapes are formed by simply folding them over. But here's something important to remember: when you fold your valances to the front, you'll see the *wrong* side of the fabric, including the hems you made in step 2. We cleverly covered the stitches at either side with a row of decorative braid, stitching it on with a zigzag stitch. Turn under the raw edge of the braid just a bit (1/4 inch or so), and begin stitching about 1 inch below the fold on the wrong side of the drape (figure 2). When you reach the raw edge, fold the trim around to the wrong side and finish the line of stitching.

FIGURE 1

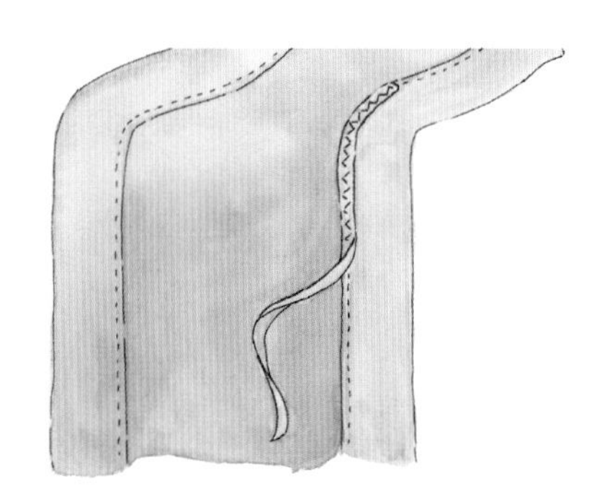

FIGURE 2

4 To stabilize (and decorate) the top of each drape, add another line of braid, placing it about 1/4 inch from the folded edge. Remember to fold the edges of the braid to the wrong side as you did in step 3.

5 Make 3-inch double hems at the bottom edges of each panel, using the same method you used in step 2.

6 Make very narrow hems at the raw edges of the self-valances by stitching 1/2 inch from the raw edge. Turn under on this line of stitching and stitch close to fold. Trim the fabric close to stitching line. Turn under 1/8 inch, encasing the raw edge. Stitch the hem in place. Press (figure 3).

7 Working with a needle and thread, backstitch the beaded trim to the edge of each self-valance, covering the very narrow hem (figure 4). To hang, attach the clips to the upper edge.

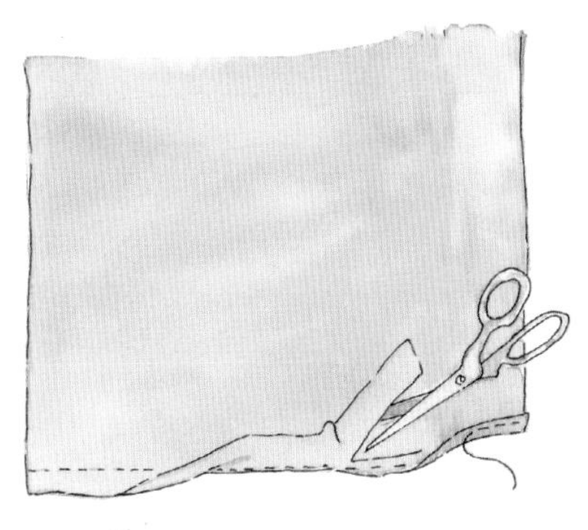

FIGURE 3

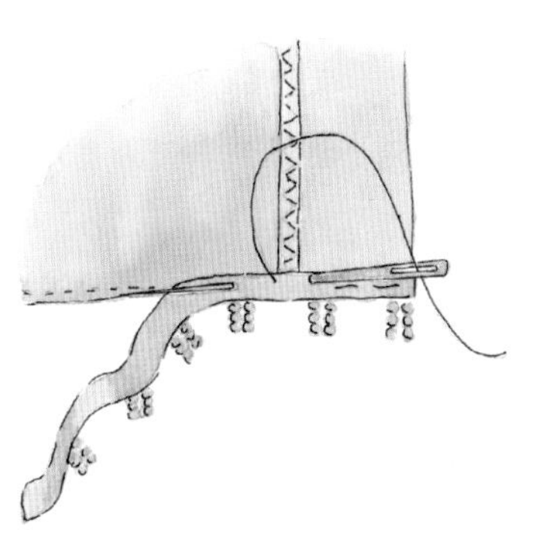

FIGURE 4

Tip

This deserves repeating (so we will): because of the construction we used in this project, the *wrong* side of the fabric will be shown as the self-valance. Keep this in mind while you're shopping for material, and make sure that the wrong side of the fabric is to your liking as well.

Hear the birds
singing?

Stylish *Swag*

Although this swag has a traditional shape, its dangling bobbles give it a playful feel. And guess what? It's reversible.

WHAT YOU NEED

- Basic curtain-making tools and supplies
- Fabric and trim to fit your window (we used 1 yard each of medium-weight cotton in two coordinating patterns—fabrics A and B, 2 yards of wide ultra-light-weight fusible web, $2\frac{1}{2}$ yards of $\frac{3}{8}$-inch ribbon, and $2\frac{1}{2}$ yards of bobble fringe)
- Matching thread
- Adhesive tape
- Templates, page 111

CURTAIN SPECS

- Window #4
- Width 1X
- 1 panel

EXPERIENCED BEGINNER

Cheat sheet for experienced beginner on page 51

HOW YOU MAKE IT

1 Although this pattern was designed for a window that's 49 inches wide, you can easily make it fit your window by altering pattern piece 1.

Determine how much narrower (or wider) you want the swag, and divide that figure in half. You'll revise the pattern from the centerline, either making it shorter (for a narrower curtain) or making it longer (for a wider curtain). For example, let's say you want to make a curtain that's 39 inches wide. That's 10 inches narrower than our pattern; half of 10 inches is 5 inches, so you'll draw a line parallel to the existing centerline that's 5 inches away into the existing pattern piece. Trim the pattern piece along the new centerline. Adjust the center dot so it's equidistant between the dots at either end.

To widen the swag, tape a big sheet of paper onto the centerline. Determine how much wider than 49 inches you want the swag. Divide that figure in half, and mark a new centerline on the extra sheet that extends that distance from the pattern piece. It should be parallel to the existing centerline. Extend the gentle curve at the bottom of the swag so it crosses the revised centerline. Adjust the center dot as indicated above.

If you need to alter the pattern, check your accuracy—*before* cutting your fabric—after you've taped both halves of the paper pattern together in step 3. Measure the pattern piece and compare it to your window measurement.

2 Measure your windows, and calculate your yardage according to the instructions on pages 18 and 19. Using the templates on page 111, enlarge the pattern pieces as directed and cut them out. Mark the dots and cut the notches.

3 Make a photocopy of pattern piece 1, cut it out, flip it, and tape it to the original, matching the centerlines. When using a directional fabric—one with a print that has an obvious top and bottom—be sure to place the pattern pieces with the upper edge facing toward the top of the fabric. Using fabric A, cut out one of pattern piece 1, cut two of pattern piece 2 (one with the pattern piece face up, and the other with the pattern piece face down, to make a left side and a right side), and cut 10 of pattern piece 3. Repeat, using fabric B. For the fusible web, cut one piece of pattern piece 1, and two of pattern piece 2.

4 Using fabric A, pin and sew pattern pieces 2 (the tails) to either side of pattern piece 1 (the swag), placing the right sides together and matching the notches. Press the seams open. Repeat with fabric B, making an identical piece from the coordinating fabric.

5 Repeat step 4 with the fusible web, but *don't* press the seams. (Using heat will not only activate the fusible web too soon, but it will ruin your iron and ironing board by covering them in melted glue. Yuck.) Pin the fusible web piece to the wrong side of fabric A (figure 1), matching all the edges, and stitch completely around the exterior, 1/4 inch from the edge. Again, don't press!

6 Begin making the tabs by pinning together one pattern piece 3 from fabric A and one pattern piece 3 from fabric B, right sides facing and matching the notches. Stitch along the notched edges. Press the seams open (figure 2).

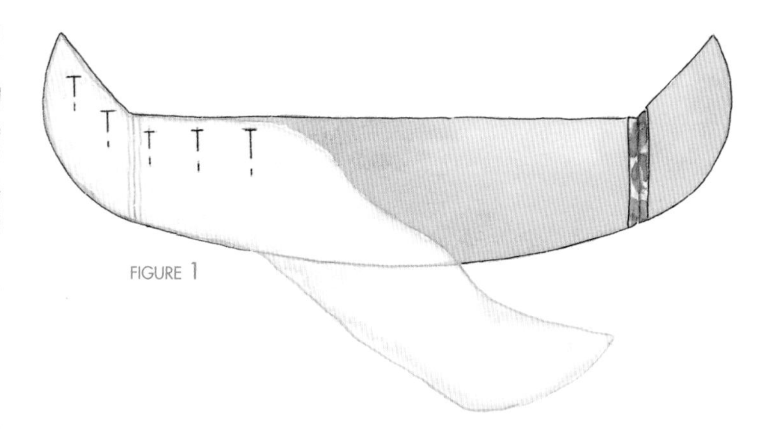

FIGURE 1

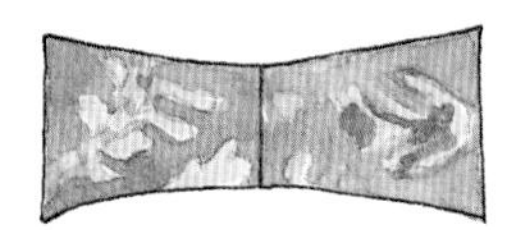

FIGURE 2

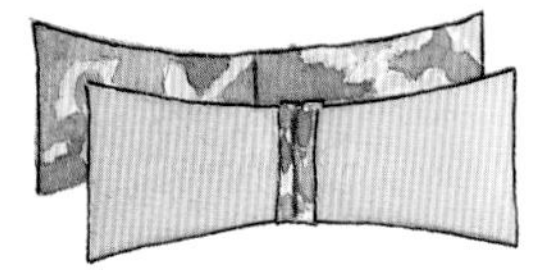

FIGURE 3

7 With right sides together, place one of the pieces made in the previous step atop another, matching the fabrics (figure 3). Stitch along both curves. Use the remaining pieces to make a total of five tabs. Notch the seams and press them open. Turn right side out and press.

8 Attach the tabs as desired, displaying either the identical fabric, the contrasting fabric, or a combination of the two. (The tab floating above figure 4 shows how the contrasting fabric will look.) To display the contrasting fabric, pin the right side of a tab made of fabric A to the right side of the swag cut from fabric B, matching circles and raw edges. Baste $^1/_4$ inch from the raw edges. Repeat with the remaining tabs.

9 Fold each tab in half, matching circles and raw edges; pin and baste (figure 4 again).

10 Put the swags cut from fabrics A and B together, right sides facing. Pin the top edges, including the tails, together. Stitch along the top edge of the swag and the tails. Notch the seam allowance where the swag and the tails are stitched together. Use a *cold* iron to press open the seam.

11 Matching the edges, pin both sides of the curtain together around the whole exterior, smoothing away any wrinkles as you proceed (figure 5). Carefully iron the entire surface to fuse the fabrics together (finally!), following the manufacturer's instructions. Trim the edges even, if necessary.

12 Pin the ribbon to the bottom edge of one side of the swag, tucking both raw ends under. Stitch. Whipstitch the bobble fringe to the other side of the swag (figure 6).

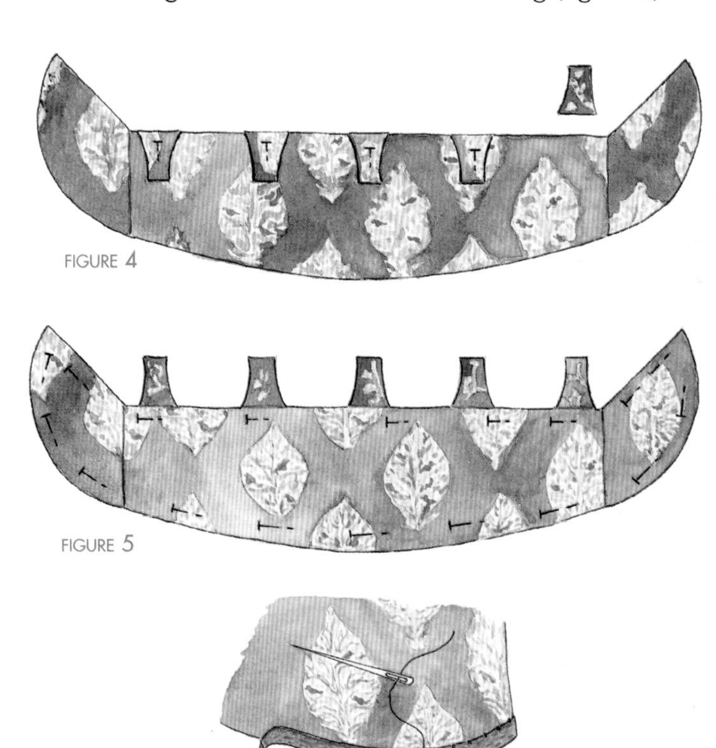

FIGURE 4

FIGURE 5

FIGURE 6

Who needs scissors?

Edgy Curtains

Add a potpourri of coordinating fabrics to embellish a sheer curtain. Use torn strips of cotton for a distressed look.

WHAT YOU NEED

Basic curtain-making tools and supplies

Fabric to fit your window (we used 5½ yards of lightweight cotton for the curtain and approximately ½ yard each of 5 coordinating fabrics for the trim)

Matching and contrasting thread

CURTAIN SPECS

Window #3

Width 1.5X

2 panels

EXPERIENCED BEGINNER

Cheat sheet for experienced beginner on page 51

HOW YOU MAKE IT

1 Measure your window, include the appropriate allowances for hems and heading, and calculate your yardage according to the instructions on pages 18 and 19. After our calculations, we found that we needed to add some additional width to span our window. So we cut two additional 10-inch-wide pieces that were the length of the main panels.

We added the following allowances to the main panel: to the width, 8 inches for the side hems; and to the length, 4 inches for the lower hem.

Cut out two panels based on your measurements. If you need additional widths, cut them also.

We also cut 14 tabs that were 6 x 9 inches each. To apply the tabs to the curtain, we needed a facing for each panel that was 3 inches by the width of our panel. So cut out two facings that are each 3 inches by the width of your panel.

For the edging strips, see the instructions in step 8.

2 To add the additional width to each panel, make a French seam. Begin by stitching the wrong sides together in a 1/4-inch seam. Trim the seam and turn the fabric inside out so the right sides are together. Stitch together in a 1/4-inch seam, encasing the raw edge. Repeat on the other panel. Press each seam to one side.

3 To make the tabs, take one piece and fold it in half lengthwise, right sides together. Stitch in a 1/2-inch seam. Turn the tab right side out, placing the seam in the center of the back of the tab. Press. If desired, topstitch along each side of the tab with contrasting thread; be sure to stitch in the same direction on each side.

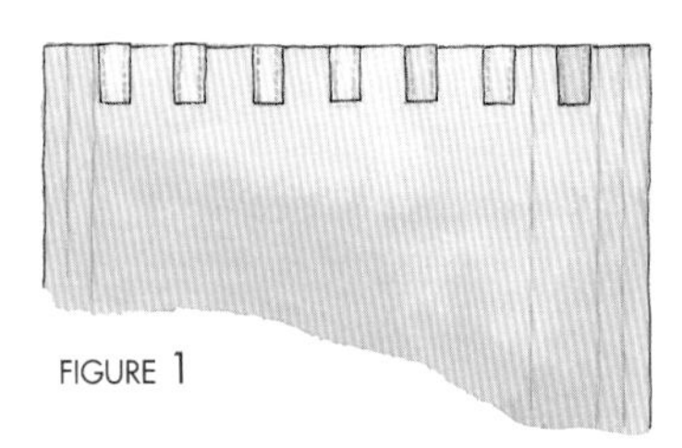

FIGURE 1

4 Determine the placement of the tabs and mark as desired. Place one at the edge of each hem allowance, and space the others approximately 6 to 8 inches apart, placing the raw edges of the tabs along the top of the curtain (figure 1). Pin and baste.

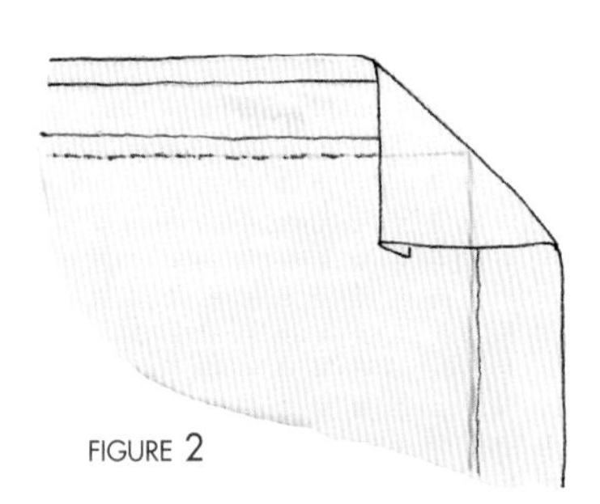

FIGURE 2

5 Prepare the lining pieces by turning under 1/2 inch on one long edge of each piece. Press. Place the lining, right sides together, on top of the tabs. Pin and stitch. Trim the seam past the first tab on each side. Press the seam toward the facing, turn the facing to the inside, and press. Open out the facing.

6 Make 2-inch double hems at the bottom and the sides of each panel, mitering the edges. Fold under 4 inches and press, then fold the raw edge in to meet the fold. Press the double hem in place, then undo the second fold. To miter, fold in the corner diagonally at the spot where the fold line and the facing seam intersect; the previous fold lines and the seam should align (figure 2). Press the corner. Trim away the excess fabric, leaving about 1/2 inch (figure 3). Fold back into the mitered edge.

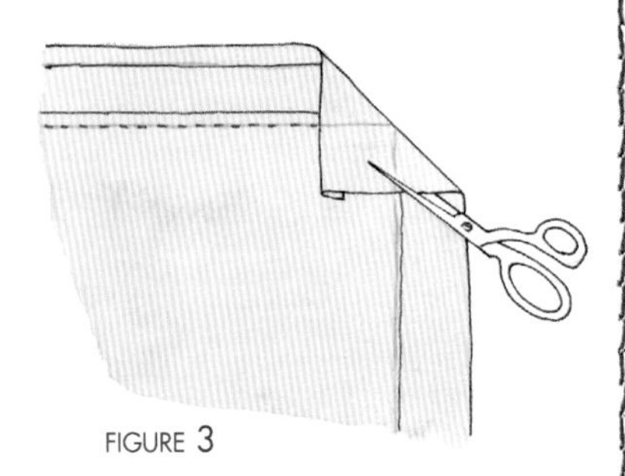

FIGURE 3

7 Miter the bottom edges as in step 6, unfolding one fold of the double hem before folding diagonally. Pin the hems in place and stitch around all sides of the curtain.

8 To prepare the distressed strips for the edge, first cut the fabrics into your desired lengths. (We used 6-inch, 9-inch, and 12-inch strips.) Then, notch every 2½ inches across the width of the fabric and rip (figure 4). The fabric will tear along the lengthwise grain.

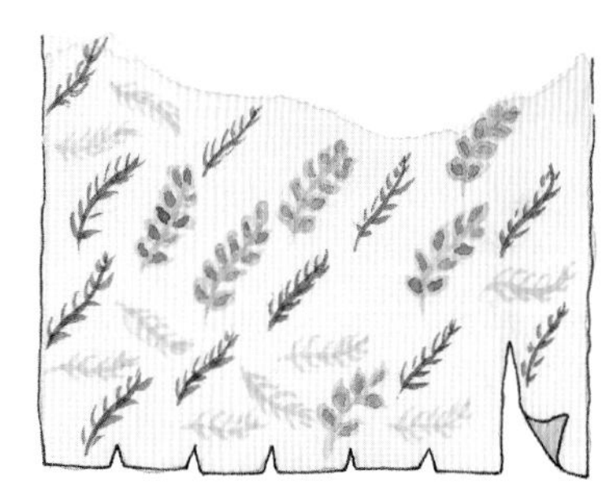

FIGURE 4

9 Pin in place on each panel, aligning the edges of the strips with the hemmed edges of the curtains. Overlap each strip slightly. At the corners, make a mock miter by folding one strip at a 45° angle and overlapping the strip underneath it (figure 5). Topstitch along the inner and outer edges of the edging strips, using a decorative stitch, if desired; we used a zigzag stitch and contrasting thread.

FIGURE 5

Simple geometry
simply beautiful

Green Medallion Curtains

Make a bold statement with appliquéd curtains that feature multiple shapes, colors, and textures.

WHAT YOU NEED

- Basic curtain-making tools and supplies
- Fabric to fit your window (we used 7 yards of neutral medium-weight cotton for the top panel, 3 yards of medium-weight colored cotton for the bottom panel, and 1/4 yard of medium-weight striped cotton for the band)
- Matching thread for the white and green cotton
- Clear nylon thread
- Approximately 1 1/4 yards of paper-backed fusible web
- 6-inch round object (such as a small plate) or a compass
- Drapery clip rings

CURTAIN SPECS

- Window #2
- Width 1.5X
- 2 panels

Cheat sheet for experienced beginner on page 51

HOW YOU MAKE IT

1 Measure your windows, include the appropriate allowances for hems and heading, and calculate your yardage according to the instructions on pages 18 and 19. We added the following allowances to each panel: to the width, 4 inches for the side hems; determine the proportion of the panels to one another (the middle and lower bands combined should be about one-quarter the length of the entire curtain) and to these dimensions, add 8 1/2 inches to the top panel for the header and seam allowance, and add 8 1/2 inches to the bottom panel for the hem and seam allowance. Our band was cut 8 inches wide and included two 1/2-inch seam allowances.

Cut out pieces for two panels based on your measurements.

2 To create the medallions, you'll cut 6-inch circles from the colored fabric. Begin by applying the fusible web to the wrong side of the fabric, following the manufacturer's instructions. Using a 6-inch round object or a compass, draw the circles onto the paper backing of the fusible web (figure 1). We cut out 13 circles per panel, for a total of 26 circles.

FIGURE 1

FIGURE 2

FIGURE 3

3 To make the centers, you'll cut 2-inch squares from the striped fabric. Apply fusible web to the fabric as in step 2, and cut out the same number of squares as you did circles. (We cut 26 again, of course.) Remove the paper backing from the squares only, leaving the paper backing in place on the circles. Following the manufacturer's instructions, fuse the squares in place in the center of each circle. Topstitch around each square, using the clear thread on top and the matching thread in the bobbin (figure 2).

4 To help with the placement of the circles on the top bands, go ahead and press the side and bottom hems in place, but don't hem them now. Press 1-inch double hems on each side by folding under 2 inches and pressing, then folding the raw edge in to meet the fold. Repeat for the heading, pressing under 8 inches for a 4-inch double hem. Spread the top bands flat and determine the placement of the medallions, arranging them inside the fold lines for the hems. (See our placement in figure 3.) Remove the paper backing from the circles one at a time, put them back in place, and pin.

5 Fuse the circles in place, following the manufacturer's instructions. Topstitch around the circles, using the invisible thread on top and the matching thread in the bobbin.

6 Switch to matching thread in the top of your machine. With right sides facing, pin and double-stitch each top band to each striped band. (We used a zigzag for the second line of stitching.) Press the seams toward the bands.

7 With right sides facing, pin and double-stitch each bottom band to each striped band as you did in step 6, pressing the seams toward the bands (figure 4).

8 Stitch down the 1-inch double hems at each side (you pressed these already, in step 4). If you'd like, switch bobbin thread to the appropriate color as you go.

9 Stitch down the 4-inch double hem at the top of each panel.

10 Make a 4-inch double hem at the bottom of each panel, using the same method you used in step 4, with the appropriate color of thread in the machine and the bobbin.

11 Clip the rings evenly across the top of each panel (figure 5).

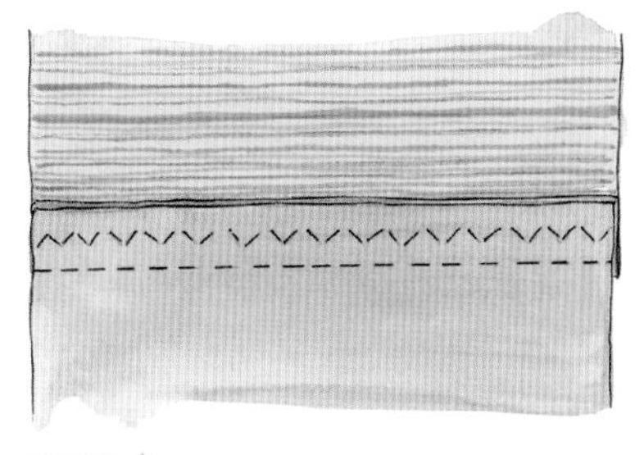

FIGURE 4

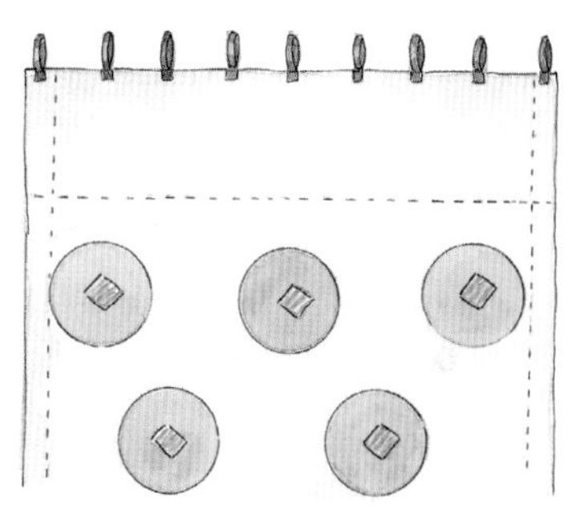

FIGURE 5

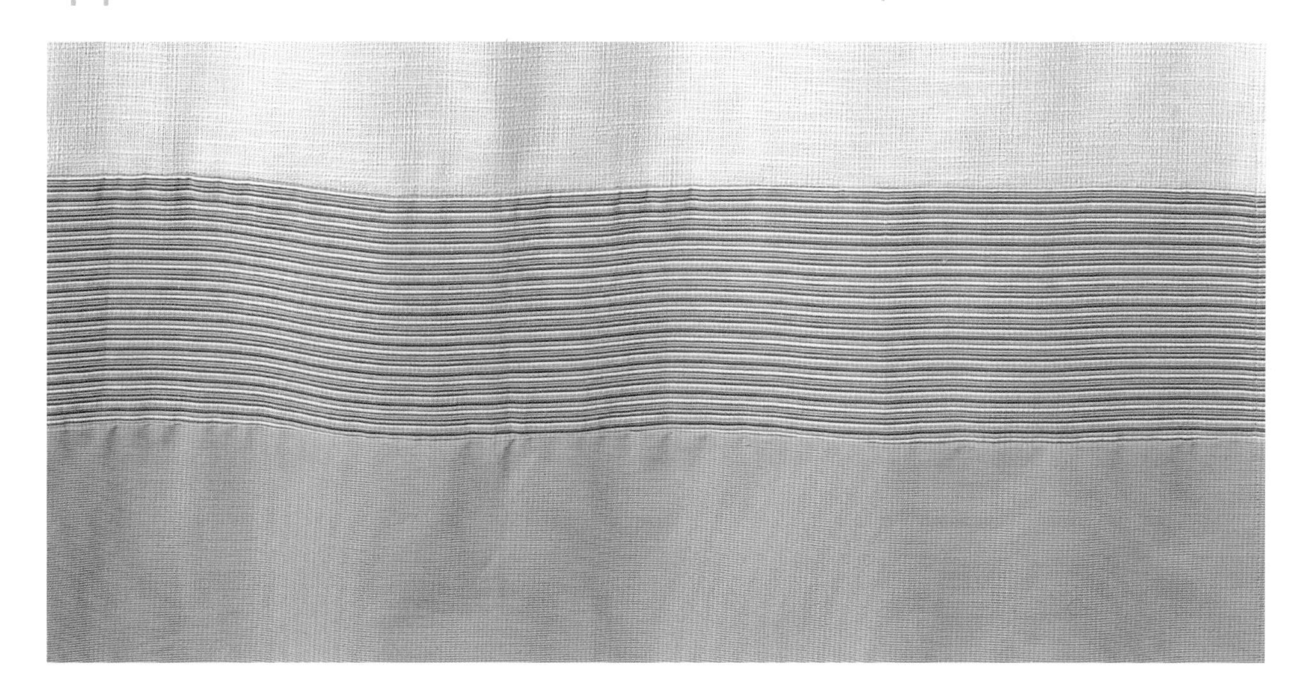

Easy. Really!

Romantic Roman Shade

Crisp fabrics accentuate the folds and gathers of this simplified Roman shade. Iron-on ring tape makes the sewing almost effortless.

HOW YOU MAKE IT

1 Measure your windows, include the appropriate allowances for hems and heading, and calculate your yardage according to the instructions on pages 18 and 19. Be sure to measure to the top of the windowsill, as in figure 1, adjusting for the size of your link rings. We added the following allowances: to the width, 4 inches for the side hems; and to the length, 16 inches for the top and bottom hems.

Cut out one panel based on your measurements. If the fabric has a dominant motif, center it before cutting.

2 Make a 1-inch double hem at each side, folding under 2 inches and pressing, then folding the raw edge in to meet the fold. Press, pin, and stitch as close to the hem edge as you can (figure 2).

FIGURE 1

FIGURE 2

WHAT YOU NEED

- Basic curtain-making tools and supplies
- Fabric to fit your window (we used 2 yards of heavyweight embroidered cotton)
- Matching thread
- Approximately 3½ yards of iron-on ring tape
- Approximately 10 yards of polyester cord
- ⅝-inch dowel, approximately as long as your window is wide
- 3 small screw eyes
- Link rings
- Ice pick
- 1 cleat
- Screwdriver and/or drill

CURTAIN SPECS

- Window #2
- Width 1X
- 1 panel

EXPERIENCED BEGINNER

Cheat sheet for experienced beginner on page 51

FIGURE 3

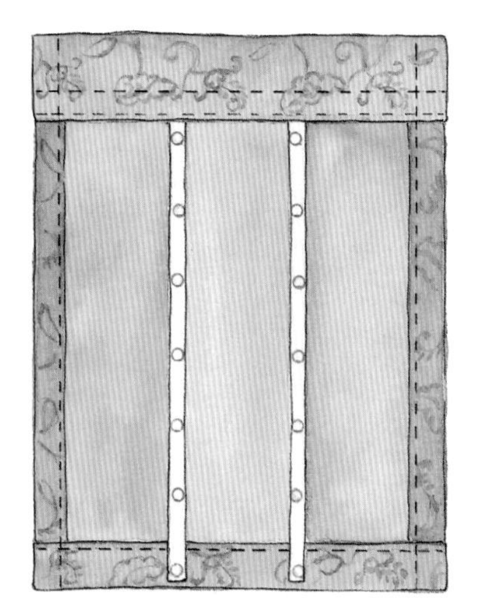

FIGURE 4

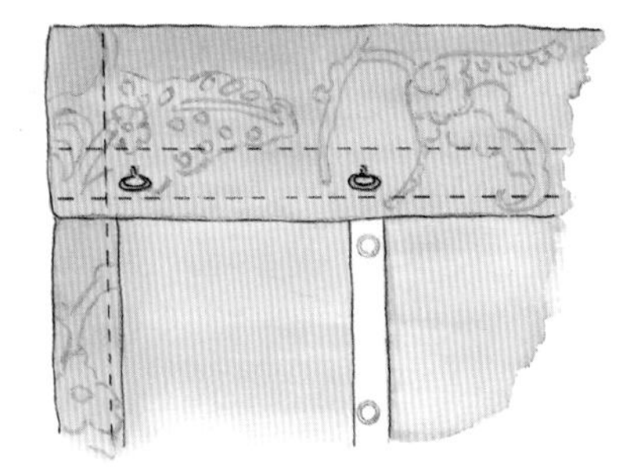

FIGURE 5

3 Make a 4-inch double hem at the top, folding under 8 inches and pressing, then folding the raw edge in to meet the fold. Press, pin, and stitch close to the edge.

4 To make a slot for the dowel, measure 1½ inches up from the stitching line you sewed in step 3 and sew another line of stitching (figure 3). Don't put the dowel in yet!

5 At the bottom, make a 4-inch double hem, using the same method you used in step 3.

6 To attach the iron-on ring tape, follow the manufacturer's instructions. Working on the wrong side of the fabric, place a length of tape about 10 inches from one side. Try to arrange it so there's a ring at the top and a ring an inch or less from the bottom. Press it in place. Repeat on the other side (figure 4).

7 Slide the dowel into the slot created in step 4 and center it across the top edge. Stitch each end shut.

8 On the wrong side, make two holes in the dowel above the strips of ring tape by pushing the ice pick through the fabric and into the wood. Insert the screw eyes. Insert another screw eye on the left side near the end of the dowel (figure 5).

9 Still working with the wrong side of the shade facing you, measure from the bottom of the right ring tape up to the screw eye; left across the top to the third screw eye at the end; and down the length of the shade. Add 4 inches to this measurement to allow for knots. Cut a piece of the cord this length.

10 Measure from the bottom of the left ring tape up to the top of the shade, then left to the end screw eye and down the length of the shade. Add 4 inches and cut another piece of the cord to this measurement.

11 Tie one end of the longer cord to the bottom ring on the right side. Run the string through all of the rings, then through the screw eyes across the top. Tie the other string to the bottom left ring tape and run it up through all the rings to the top, then to the left (figure 6).

12 Stitch the link rings on by hand (figure 7), evenly spacing them across the top of the shade and making sure both rings at the ends are close to the edges. Use a doubled length of thread and loop the stitches around at least 10 times to ensure strength.

13 Hang the shade in place and let the strings hang loose. At the upper right side, where the cords come through the last screw eye, tie them together in a knot. Braid the cord if desired. Install the cleat in your window frame according to the manufacturer's instructions. Use it to tie off the cord and hold the shade in the appropriate position.

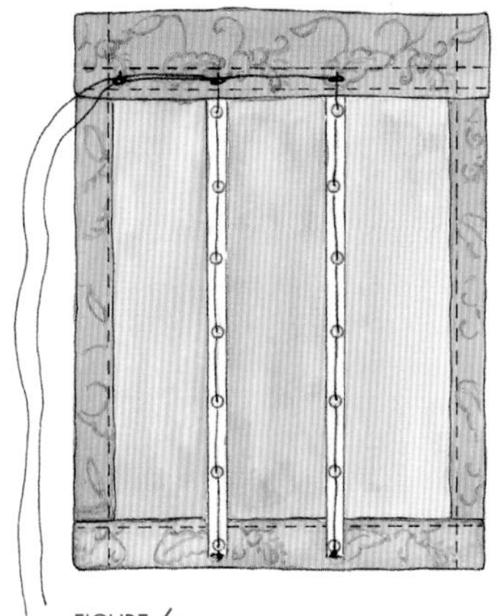

FIGURE 6

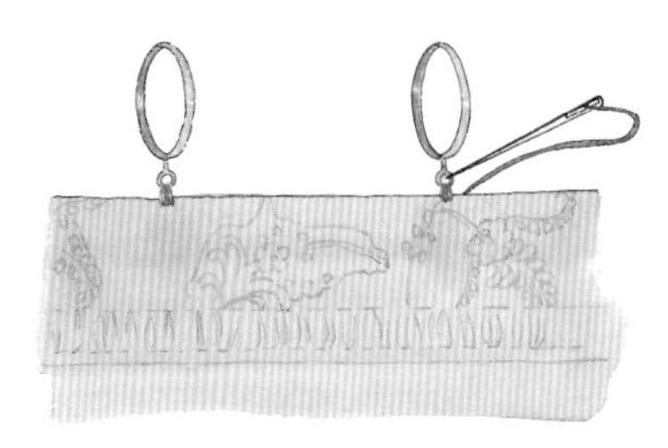

FIGURE 7

Luxury without fuss.

Pleated Curtains

These curtains will dress any room in splendor. Let them puddle on the floor for added impact.

HOW YOU MAKE IT

1 Measure your window, include the appropriate allowances for hems and headings, and calculate your yardage according to the instructions on pages 18 and 19.

2 We're going to teach you the quick-and-dirty method of pleating curtains made from 60-inch-wide fabric. It does involve some math (just a little bit) to figure out how much of the 60 inches will be folded into the pleats so you end up with your desired finished width. Here's what to do; we've also got a chart of these calculations on page 101.

Let's say your finished panels should be 30 inches wide. Next, decide how many pleats you want—how about 10? Between the pleats, you'll have spaces; you'll have one more space than you have pleats, so you'll have 11 spaces. Divide your finished panel width (30 inches) by the number of spaces (11); this tells you how far apart each pleat will be. Round off this figure to the nearest 1/8 inch (2 3/4 inches). Then, subtract the finished width (30 inches) from the width of the fabric (60 inches), which leaves 30 inches. Subtract 2 more inches for the hem allowances on the sides—1 inch on each side (30 inches – 2 inches = 28 inches). So, we have 28 inches of fabric that needs to be taken up in the 10 pleats to reduce our 60-inch fabric to a finished width of 30 inches.

We're just about done! Divide 28 inches by the number of pleats (10), round off to the nearest 1/8 inch again, and you have

WHAT YOU NEED

Basic curtain-making tools and supplies

Fabric to fit your window (we used 6 yards of 60-inch-wide rayon/polyester blend)

Matching thread

CURTAIN SPECS

Window #3

Width 2X

2 panels

EXPERIENCED BEGINNER

Cheat sheet for experienced beginner on page 51

the depth of the pleats—2¾ inches. After you do this figuring, write down your pleat space (2¾ inches in our example) and your pleat depth (2¾ inches in our example). You'll need these figures in step 3.

Trust me—this all works out. But because you'll be converting decimals from a calculator to fractions on a tape measure and rounding off the numbers, you may have a bit more fabric on one end or the other. When you make the second panel, you'll duplicate what you've done on the first panel, only in reverse orientation. So you can balance the panels by placing the longer ends at each side or let them adjoin each other in the center.

If this is your first time with pleats (or a calculator), it's probably wise to test your math by making the pleats on a piece of inexpensive muslin or by making folds in a strip of paper—the fabric or paper should be cut to 60 inches, the width of your fabric. You can also play with the number of pleats and the space between them, of course.

After we calculated the pleats as above, we added the following allowances to each panel: to the length, 5 inches for the rod pocket casing, 6 inches for the lower hem, and 6 inches for puddling.

Cut two panels based on your measurements.

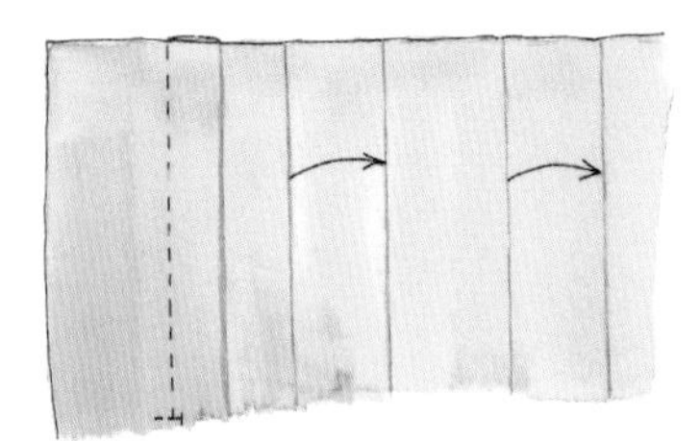

FIGURE 1

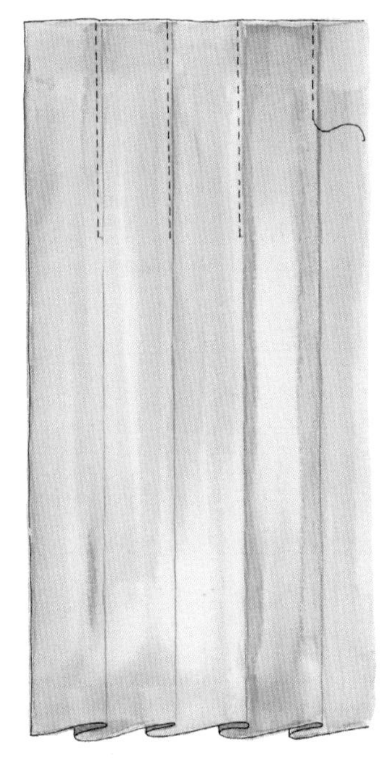

FIGURE 2

3 On one of the panels, begin marking the pleats 1 inch from the edge (your side hem allowance). From that spot, mark a series of lines that indicate your pleat space, then your pleat depth, and continue this pattern across the curtain, alternating the distances. (In our make-believe example from step 2, we would have marked at 1 inch, then 2¾ inches away, and 2¾ inches away, and so on. Our distances happen to be the same, but yours might not.) Make the pleats as in figure 1, folding the fabric from the pleat space marks to the pleat depth marks. Stitch together where the lines meet; our pleats are stitched down about one-fifth the length of the curtains. On the right side of the curtains, topstitch along the pleats (figure 2).

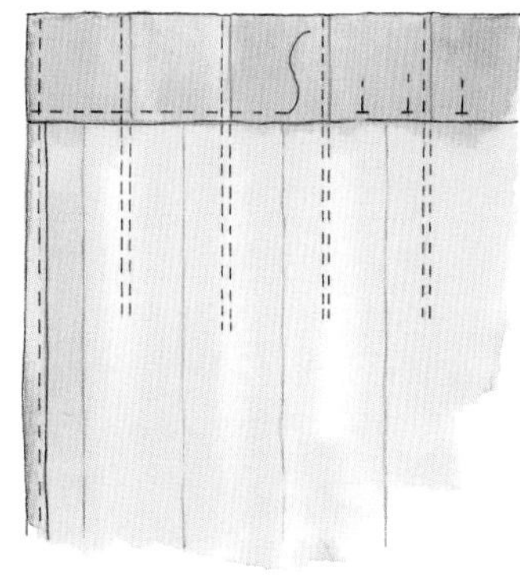

FIGURE 3

4 Mirror step 3 on the other panel so the pleats face the opposite direction.

5 Make 1/2-inch double hems at each side, folding under 1 inch and pressing, then folding the raw edge in to meet the fold. Press, pin, and stitch.

6 Create the casing at the top of each panel. Press under 5 inches, and then turn under 1/2 inch on the raw edge. Press. Pin in place and stitch (figure 3).

7 Make a 3-inch double hem at the bottom of each panel, folding under 6 inches and pressing, then folding the raw edge in to meet the fold. Press, pin, and stitch.

Why?

Why 60-inch fabric? Actually, it doesn't have to be. You can use our formula to calculate pleat space and depth for any width you need. It could be wider, if you seam panels together, or narrower (so long as you have enough fabric to pleat). For example, if you wanted a very lush, full curtain, stitch two 60-inch widths together, and begin your calculations with the final width of your fabric piece.

Pleat Calculator

________ FABRIC WIDTH

________ FINISHED PANEL WIDTH

________ # OF PLEATS

________ # OF SPACES

________ PANEL WIDTH

÷ ________ # OF SPACES

________ PLEAT SPACE

________ FABRIC WIDTH

\- ________ FINISHED PANEL WIDTH

\- ________ SIDE HEM ALLOWANCE

________ INCHES TO BE PLEATED

÷ ________ # OF PLEATS

________ PLEAT DEPTH

Simply irresistible.

Elegant Silk Draperies

When you're ready for a sophisticated look, consider these drapes. Pleating tape makes the decorative heading quick and easy.

WHAT YOU NEED

- Basic curtain-making tools and supplies
- Fabric, trim, and accessories to fit your window (we used 4 yards of blue silk for the top panels, 2 yards of green silk for the bottom panels, 6 yards of lining fabric, 3 yards of tassel fringe, and 4 yards of pleating tape)
- Thread to match each color of silk
- Clear nylon thread
- Tape hooks
- Link rings

CURTAIN SPECS

- Window #3
- Width 1.5X
- 2 panels

EXPERIENCED BEGINNER

Cheat sheet for experienced beginner on page 51

HOW YOU MAKE IT

1 Measure your windows, include the appropriate allowances for hems and heading, and calculate your yardage according to the instructions on pages 18 and 19 and the instructions with your pleating tape. (See *Why?* on page 105.) We added the following allowances to each panel: to the width, 3 inches for the side hems; determine the proportion of the panels to one another (our bottom piece is roughly one-quarter the length of the top piece), and to these dimensions, add 8½ inches to the top panel for the heading and a seam allowance, and add 8½ inches to the bottom panel for the hem and a seam allowance. Purchase the same amount of lining fabric as curtain fabric.

Cut out pieces for two panels based on your measurements. For the lining, see the instructions in step 3.

2 With right sides together, stitch the top and bottom pieces of each panel. Press the seam open. Cut a piece of fringe to the width of the panel. On the right side of the panel, pin it over the seam. Machine stitch the fringe in place along each edge (figure 1).

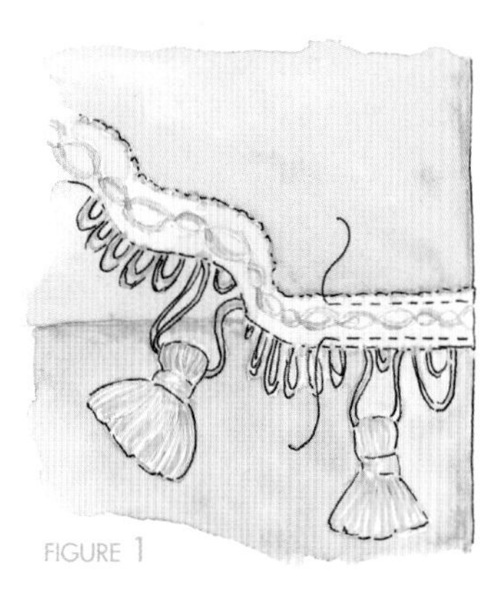
FIGURE 1

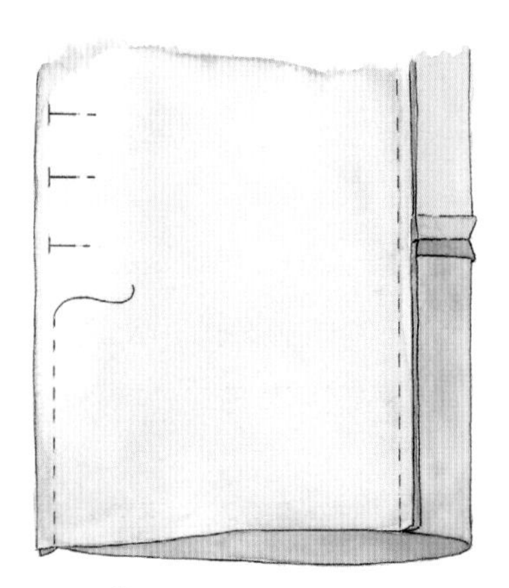
FIGURE 2

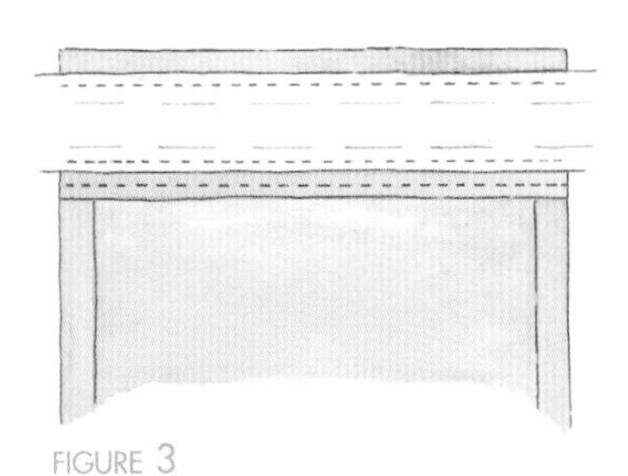
FIGURE 3

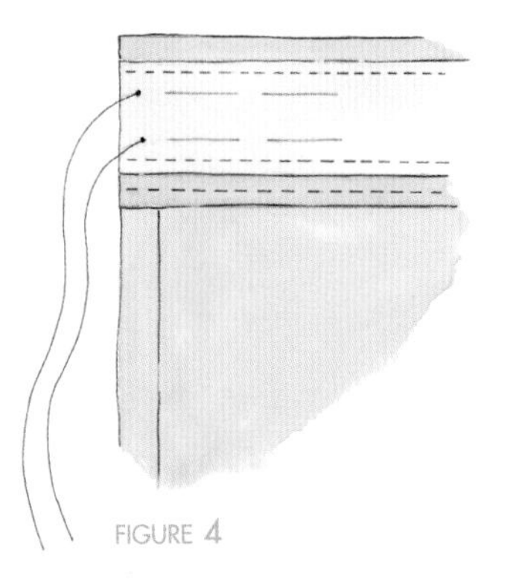
FIGURE 4

3 For the lining, measure the panels you made in step 2, and subtract 4 inches from the width and 3 inches from the length. Cut two lining panels to this measurement.

4 Place each lining and curtain right sides together, aligning the top edge and one side edge. Pin and stitch the side seam. Now, pin and stitch the other side edge (figure 2). You'll have more of the curtain material than the lining material, by design. Turn right side out. Press the long edges, leaving a 1-inch overlap of the fabric on the wrong side.

5 Make a 4-inch double hem at the top edge of each panel; fold under 8 inches and press, then fold the raw edge in to meet the fold. Press, pin, and stitch. Cut the pleating tape to the width of your curtain, adding an extra inch or two on each side. Follow the manufacturer's instructions to apply the pleating tape; with the type we used, we centered the tape and stitched along both edges, following stitching lines printed on the pleating tape. There are strings along the edges that pull the tape into pleats, so be careful not to stitch over the pull strings (figure 3).

6 At one end of the pleating tape, tie a double knot in each string (figure 4). Pull the strings simultaneously from the other end. Keep pulling and creating the folds as you go until you have all the pleats in place, making sure the area between the folds stays flat. When you're satisfied with the pleats, knot each string. Repeat on the other panel.

7 On the right side, make a small tack at the base of each pleat (figure 5).

8 Place the tape hooks at each pleat (figure 6). The kind we used are inserted through the back of the tape and flipped around to secure.

9 Make a 4-inch double hem at the bottom, using the same method you used in step 5, stitching the curtain over the lining.

10 Rather than place these drapes on a sliding track, we used simple link rings to attach them to the curtain rod.

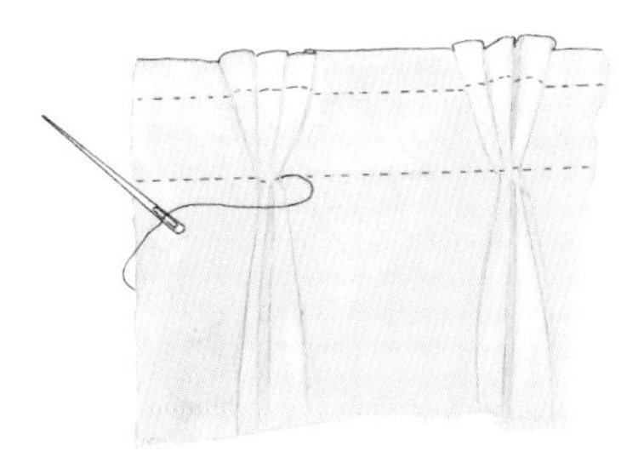

FIGURE 5

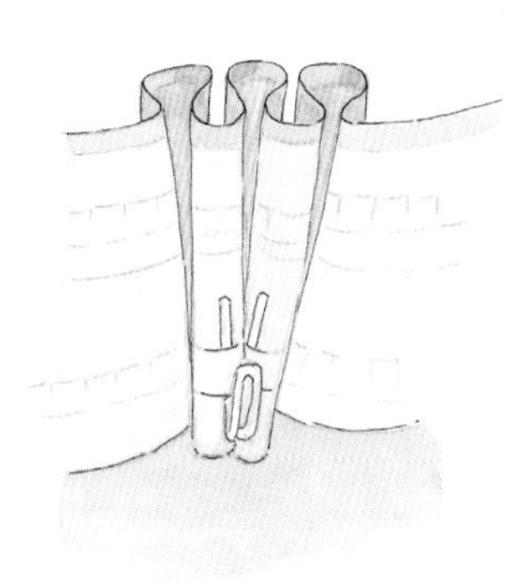

FIGURE 6

Why?

While we've given you general instructions for using pleating tape, be sure to follow the manufacturer's instructions when you're using these kinds of products, as the directions and yardage requirements may vary from company to company.

Embellishment Techniques

Here's your special bonus section! If you'd like to explore some additional ways to adorn your curtains, try these simple techniques.

Sewing Techniques

Some of the stitches in this section and the embroidery section are interchangeable, as they can be used in sewing or embroidery.

APPLIQUÉ. The applying of one fabric layer to another. You can stitch appliqués by machine, using a satin stitch, or by hand, using practically any of the stitches described in this section.

BLANKET STITCH. This loop stitch can be decorative or functional. After anchoring the thread near the fabric edge from the wrong side, insert the needle again from the right side so it's perpendicular to the fabric edge. Pass the needle over the thread and pull, repeating for each successive stitch (figure 1).

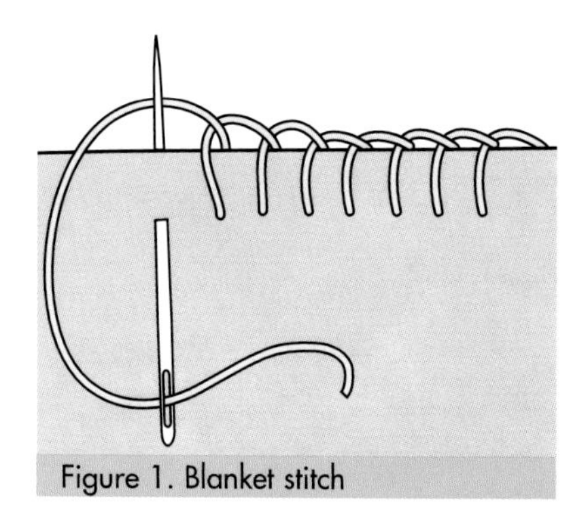

Figure 1. Blanket stitch

SATIN STITCH. In machine stitching, make a satin stitch with zigzag stitch set to a short length, so the stitches are very close together. For hand stitching, see the Embroidery Stitches section on page 108.

TOPSTITCH. Machine stitching on the right side of the garment that follows an edge or a seam.

WHIPSTITCH. A utilitarian slanted hand stitch where the needle is inserted perpendicular to the fabric edge (figure 2).

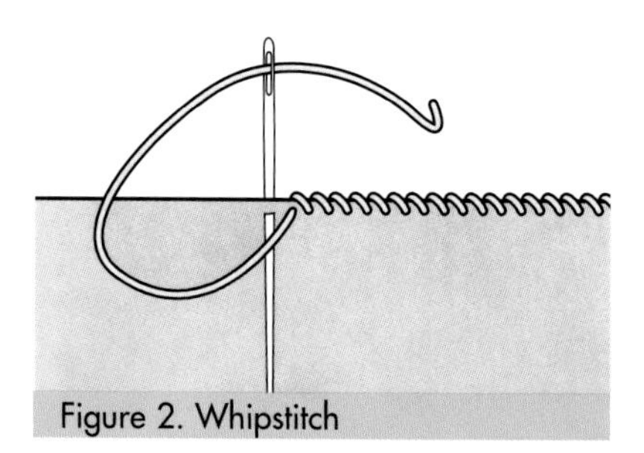

Figure 2. Whipstitch

Sequin Techniques

There are several different ways to attach flashy little sequins to your curtains. The easiest way is to simply stitch up through the center and back down around the edge of the sequin a few times, but there are some fancier ways, too.

Figure 3. Sequin stitching

WITH A BEAD. If you prefer to hide the thread, add a bead in the center of the sequin. Stitch through the center of the sequin from the wrong side, add the bead, and stitch down through the center (figure 3).

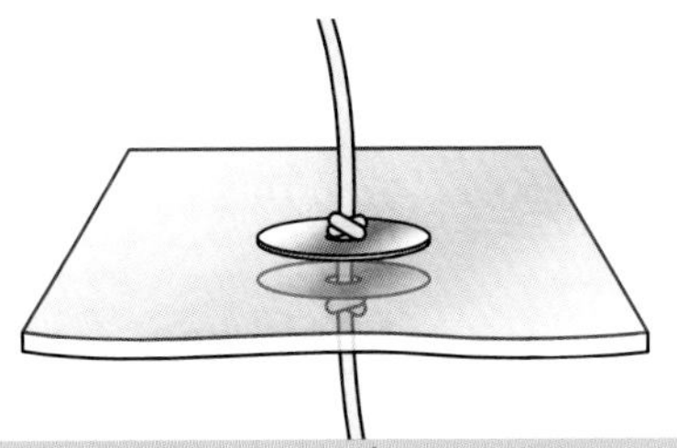

Figure 4. Sequin stitching

WITH A DECORATIVE THREAD. If you'd like for the thread to be part of the embellishment, stitch down through the center of the sequin, leaving the knot and tail visible. If you wanted, you could add a sequin to both sides, creating some additional sparkle (figure 4).

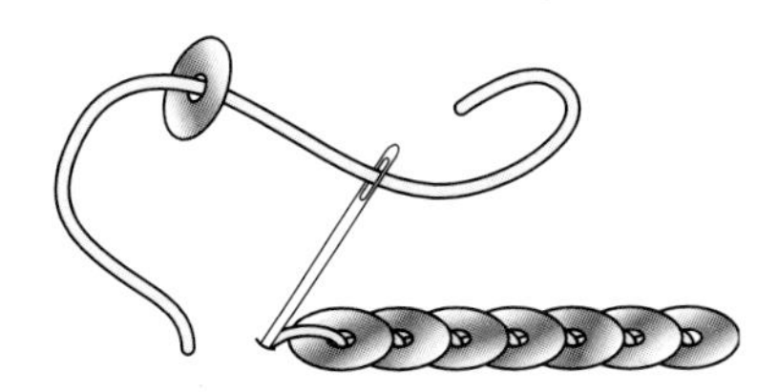

Figure 5. Sequin stitching

IN A LINE. If you'd like to add a line of sequins, use backstitches to secure the sequins (figure 5). This technique is very similar to the bead technique described below.

Beading Techniques

Simple bead embroidery can add dazzling highlights to your curtain. To begin, you need only thread, a needle, and, of course, beads. There are specialized threads and needles for beading, but clear nylon thread can work, too. Any fine needle that will pass through the beads can be used as well.

Here are a couple of easy techniques.

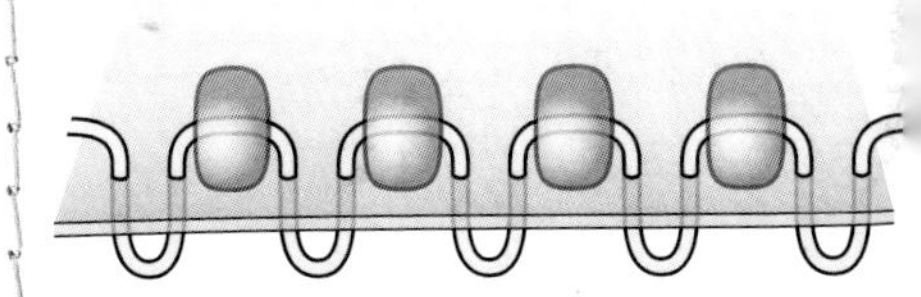

Figure 6. Single stitch

SINGLE STITCH. This is basically a running stitch with a bead in each stitch. Each time the needle emerges from the wrong side of the fabric, slide a bead onto it and down to the fabric. Push the needle through to the wrong side just at the edge of the bead (figure 6).

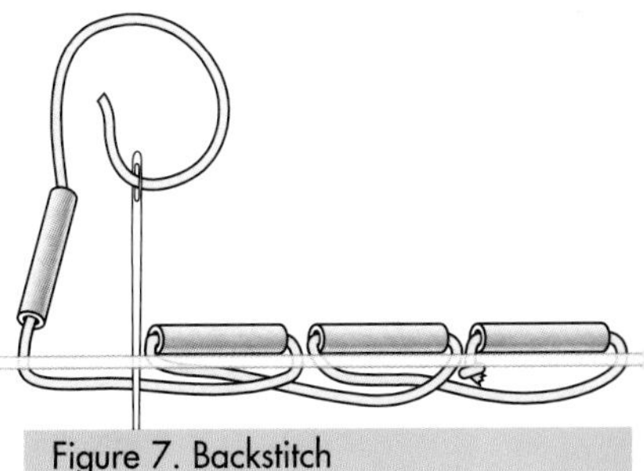

Figure 7. Backstitch

BACKSTITCH. Add a line of beads using the backstitch. This stitch is like backstitch in regular sewing, with a bead added. To add a single bead, slide a bead onto the needle each time it emerges from the fabric and insert the needle at the edge of the previous bead. Begin the next stitch one bead's length away (figure 7).

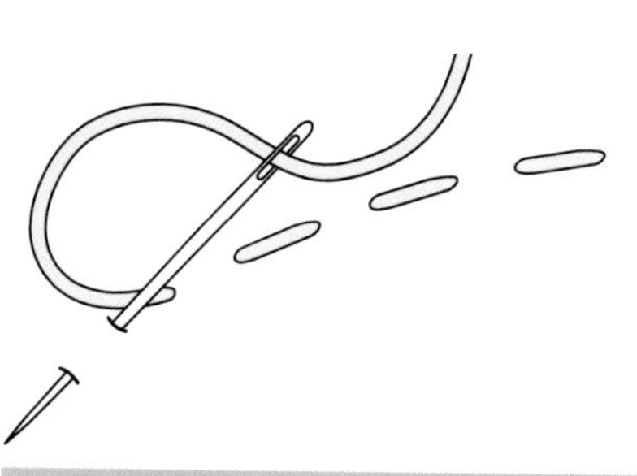

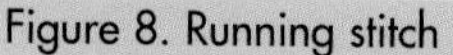

Figure 8. Running stitch

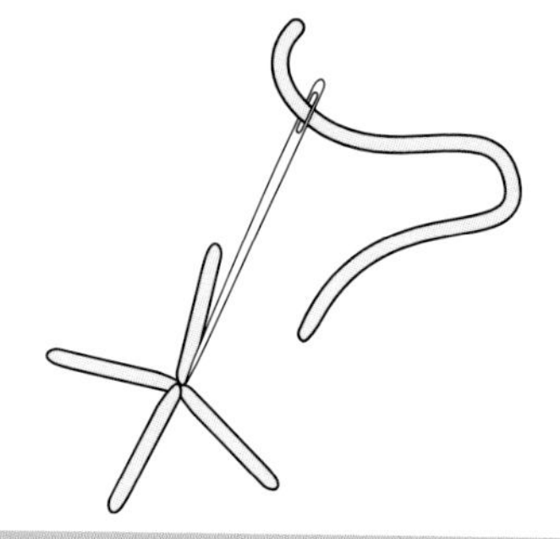

Figure 9. Straight stitch

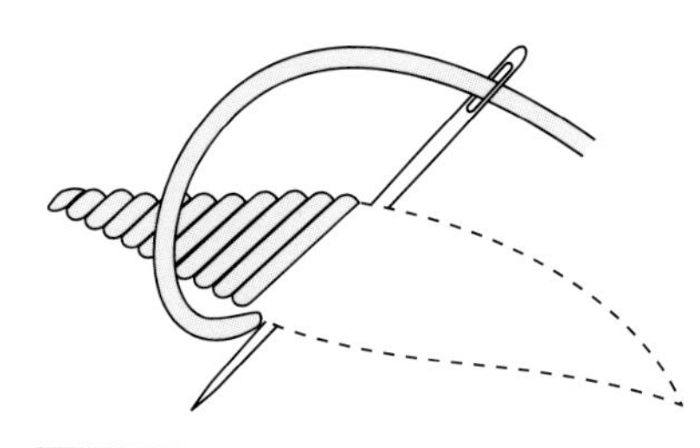

Figure 10. Satin stitch

Embroidery Techniques

Embroidery is an age-old embellishment technique. The tools and supplies you need for hand embroidery are few: floss, needles, an embroidery hoop, and perhaps a marking tool or quilter's tape. Usually, you'll want to separate the floss so you're working with three or fewer strands. Carefully place your curtain into an embroidery hoop for stability, if possible, and mark the placement of your stitches if necessary.

Here are some basic embroidery stitches.

RUNNING STITCH. An easy stitch to execute, the running stitch is made by simply weaving the needle through the garment at evenly spaced intervals (figure 8).

STRAIGHT STITCH. Use a series of straight stitches to create a motif (figure 9).

SATIN STITCH. Satin stitch is composed of parallel rows of straight stitches (figure 10).

CROSS-STITCH. Cross-stitch is a series of diagonal stitches. The finished stitches can be touching one another or separated by space, as desired (figure 11).

FRENCH KNOT. The elegant French knot is created by wrapping the thread around the needle once or twice (or thrice!), then inserting it back into the fabric at the point where the needle emerged (figure 12).

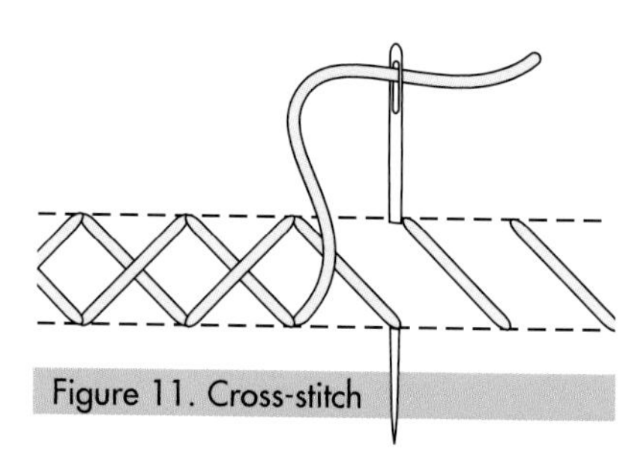

Figure 11. Cross-stitch

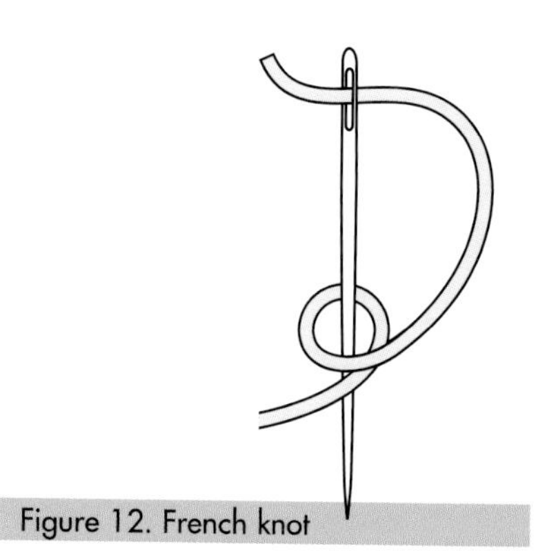

Figure 12. French knot

Metric Conversion Chart

INCHES	MILLIMETERS (MM)/ CENTIMETERS (CM)
⅛	3 mm
3⁄16	5 mm
¼	6 mm
5⁄16	8 mm
⅜	9.5 mm
7⁄16	1.1 cm
½	1.3 cm
9⁄16	1.4 cm
⅝	1.6 cm
11⁄16	1.7 cm
¾	1.9 cm
13⁄16	2.1 cm
⅞	2.2 cm
15⁄16	2.4 cm
1	2.5 cm
1½	3.8 cm
2	5 cm
2½	6.4 cm
3	7.6 cm
3½	8.9 cm
4	10.2 cm
4½	11.4 cm
5	12.7 cm
5½	14 cm
6	15.2 cm
6½	16.5 cm
7	17.8 cm
7½	19 cm
8	20.3 cm
8½	21.6 cm
9 (¼ yard)	22.9 cm
9½	24.1 cm
10	25.4 cm
10½	26.7 cm
11	27.9 cm
11½	29.2 cm
12	30.5 cm
12½	31.8 cm
13	33 cm
13½	34.3 cm
14	35.6 cm
14½	36.8 cm
15	38.1 cm

INCHES	MILLIMETERS (MM)/ CENTIMETERS (CM)
15½	39.4 cm
16	40.6 cm
16½	41.9 cm
17	43.2 cm
17½	44.5 cm
18 (½ yard)	45.7 cm
18½	47 cm
19	48.3 cm
19½	49.5 cm
20	50.8 cm
20½	52 cm
21	53.3
21½	54.6
22	55 cm
22½	57.2 cm
23	58.4 cm
23½	59.7 cm
24	61 cm
24½	62.2 cm
25	63.5 cm
25½	64.8 cm
26	66 cm
26½	67.3 cm
27	68.6 cm
27½	69.9 cm
28	71.1 cm
28½	72.4 cm
29	73.7 cm
29½	74.9 cm
30	76.2 cm
30½	77.5 cm
31	78.7 cm
31½	80 cm
32	81.3 cm
32½	82.6 cm
33	83.8 cm
33½	85 cm
34	86.4 cm
34½	87.6 cm
35	88.9 cm
35½	90.2 cm
36 (1 yard)	91.4 cm

Designer Biographies

KELLEDY FRANCIS is an artist and seamstress working on her own line of fashion. Kelledy holds a B.F.A. in fiber arts from the Maryland Institute, College of Art, and an M.F.A. in integrated media from Western Carolina University. She lives and works in Asheville, North Carolina, as a custom clothier and garment alterations specialist. See Kelledy's curtains on pages 60, 63, and 98.

The artistic endeavors of **JOAN K. MORRIS** have led her down many successful creative paths, including ceramics and costume design. Joan has contributed projects for numerous Lark books, including *Exquisite Embellishments for Your Clothes* (2006), *Sew Cool, Sew Simple: Stylish Skirts* (2006), and *Fun & Fabulous Pillows to Sew* (2006). Joan's curtains are on pages 72, 75, 90, 94, and 102.

NATHALIE MORNU has made projects for numerous Lark books, including *Exquisite Embellishments for Your Clothes* (2006), *Sew Cool, Sew Simple: Stylish Skirts* (2006), and *Fun & Fabulous Pillows to Sew* (2006). She lives in Asheville, North Carolina, but looks for shiny things wherever she may be. See Nathalie's curtains on pages 69 and 82.

Glossary

BACKSTITCH. A stitch worked from left to right; each new stitch ends at the left side of the previous stitch.

BASTING STITCH. A long, straight stitch used to hold pieces together temporarily or to gather.

BIAS. The diagonal between the lengthwise and crosswise threads in woven fabric. Fabric has the most stretch in this direction.

CASING. A fabric channel, or pocket, stitched into the top of the curtain through which the rod will be inserted.

CURTAIN. An unlined rectangle of fabric that dresses a window, providing decoration and privacy. *See also* drapery.

DOUBLE HEM. A hem made of two folds of equal size.

DRAPERY. A tailored, full-length window treatment that is lined with fabric; often, draperies also feature a third layer of interlining. *See also* curtain.

DROP. The length of the curtain.

EASE. Ease means to adjust the length of one piece to fit another; easestitching with basting stitches is used when joining two pieces that are slightly unequal in length.

EASESTITCHING. See ease.

FACING. A separate piece of fabric used to finish an edge.

FREE ARM. A narrow sewing surface created when a removable accessory tray is detached from the sewing machine.

GATHERS. Gathers are created by pulling a length of fabric into a series of folds.

GRAIN. The direction of the threads in woven fabric.

HEADER. A decorative ruffle that extends above the curtain rod. Sometimes also called the heading.

HEADING. The top of the curtain that's attached to, or hung from, the curtain rod or pole; often decorative as well as functional.

HEMSTITCH. A hand stitch that catches a thread of the garment and a thread of a folded edge.

INTERFACING. A special fabric that's used to stabilize parts of a curtain.

NARROW HEM. A narrow folded hem stitched into place by hand or machine.

NOTIONS. All the other items you need to sew in addition to the fabric.

PIVOT. To turn the fabric to change direction while sewing.

PRESS. To move the iron across the fabric by pressing it up and down, as opposed to sliding it.

SEAM ALLOWANCE. This is the amount of space between the edge of the fabric and the seamline.

SEAMLINE. The stitching line.

SELVAGE. The finished border on a length of fabric.

STRAIGHT STITCH. The basic sewing machine stitch.

TACK. A straight stitch to join interior layers of fabric, such as securing a facing to a seam allowance.

TAKE-UP. The amount that a rod-pocket curtain is shortened by the diameter of the rod.

Templates

STYLISH SWAG, page 82. Enlarge 400%

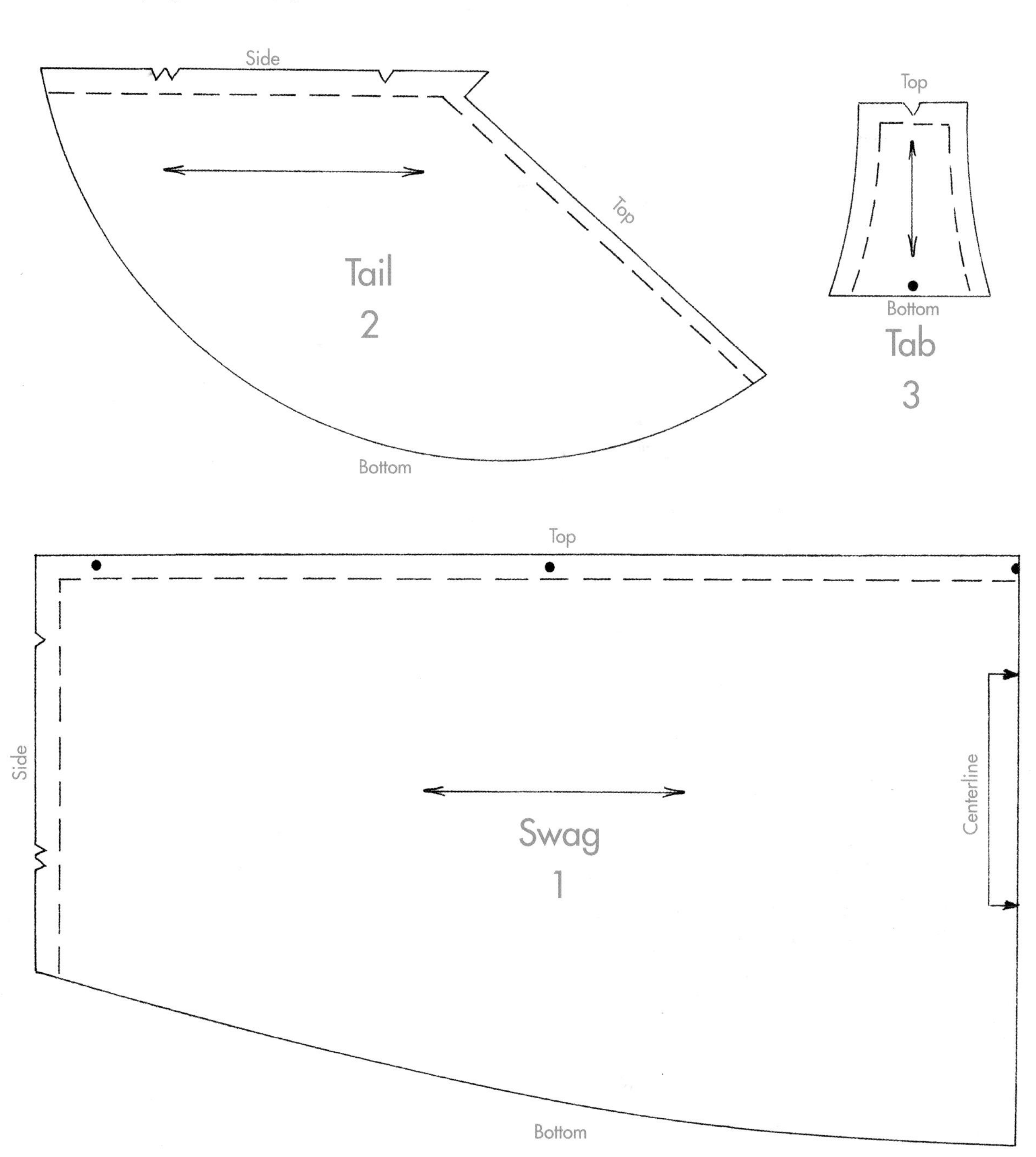

Acknowledgments

A curtain seems like such a simple thing, doesn't it? But it took a hive full of very creative worker bees to create this book.

To the curtain sewers—Joanie, Kelledy, and Nathalie—I extend my deepest appreciation. They've been with me through the creation of three other learn-to-sew books, and I'm truly grateful for their talent and good humor. (The talent part is great, but the good humor is indispensable.) Read a bit more about these creative women on page 109.

Although I didn't think it was possible, art director Stacey Budge and photographer Stewart O'Shields have surpassed the work they did on the last book we made together, *Fun & Fabulous Pillows to Sew.* The photo shoot was a testament to their creativity, ingenuity, and collective ability to count to ten and take a deep breath. (If only you knew.) They were joined in this endeavor by stylist extraordinaire Skip Wade, who made everything look beautiful, and photographer's assistant Katie Humphries, who made everything else happen. The photography turned out to be fantastic, and Stacey used it to design what I hope you'll agree is a hip sewing book.

Thanks to the gracious folks at LG Gallery (Kim Dills and John Arseneault), who allowed us to use their fabulous space for the shoot, and to artist Richard Conn, whose striking paintings in the gallery serve as the backdrop for several of our photographs. Thanks also to Terra Nostra Décor (Luis Serapo) for the loan of many beautiful props. All of the businesses mentioned above are in Asheville, North Carolina.

Finally, thanks to Steve, for not expecting too much out of me for quite some time now. (As you've probably guessed, this is an old family joke, and I assure you he knows what it means.) It's not easy to live with someone who's been writing and sewing constantly for, oh, about two years now, and I love him for it.

Index